In the Quiet of This Moment

In the Quiet of This Moment

A WOMAN'S PRAYER JOURNAL
WITH SELECTED QUOTES FROM
INSPIRATIONAL WRITERS

Laurel Oke Logan

BETHANY HOUSE PUBLISHERS
Minneapolis, Minnesota 55438

Every attempt has been made to give appropriate acknowledgment to the authors of the material used in this book. If there is an error or omission, please contact the author through Bethany House Publishers.

Book insides designed by Sherry Paavola.

Published by Bethany House Publishers
A Ministry of Bethany Fellowship, Inc.
11300 Hampshire Avenue South
Minneapolis, Minnesota 55438

Printed in the United States of America

Library of Congress Cataloging-in-Publication Data

Logan, Laurel Oke.
    In the quiet of this moment : a women's prayer journal with selected quotes from inspirational writers / Laurel Oke Logan.
        p. cm.

    1. Women—Prayer-books and devotions—English. 2. Devotional calendars. I. Title.
BV4844.L64   1995
242'.643—dc20   95–22966
ISBN 1–55661–611–2   CIP

There seems no more obvious choice
to me than to lovingly dedicate
this book about prayer
to the two people in my life
who most clearly demonstrated its importance.

To my father, who made breakfast each morning
with a round red mark on his forehead —
formed during his time of morning prayer
where he had leaned his head upon his hand
as he knelt to pray.
He was not even aware how thoroughly
he demonstrated, more than just taught,
daily prayer.

And to my mother, whose life choices
were consistently prayer focused.
And whose prayers of protection I have truly "felt"
blanketing my own family when our
two-year-old daughter was lost by a babysitter,
when a serious accident involved all four of my children
while I was thousands of miles away,
and during all manner of potential tragedies.
God heard her prayers and was a shield around us all.

I thank God for my parents and for
hearing their prayers.

Laurel Oke Logan

is a homemaker and the best-selling author
of her mother's biography, *Janette Oke:
A Heart for the Prairie*, and the SpringSong
book, *Gillian*. She and her husband have
four children and live in Indiana.

Monthly Outline

January
Worship — Joni Eareckson Tada

February
Love of God — Edith Schaeffer

March
Forgiveness/Repentance — Corrie ten Boom

April
Our Savior — Dorothy L. Sayers

May
Holy Spirit — Catherine Marshall

June
Limitations — Annie Chapman

July
Suffering — Dale Evans Rogers

August
Faith — Hannah Whitall Smith

September
Anger — Patsy Clairmont

October
Intercession — Janette Oke

November
Thankfulness — Elisabeth Elliot

December
Detours — B.J. Hoff

Introduction

Prayer. It is a word that summons a myriad of images to our minds. Is it mystical? Is it transcendental? Is it harnessing God's power for our own gain? Is it necessary?

Today there is great confusion as to what prayer is, in the church and even more so in the world around us. And yet, the answer can be explained so simply. It is speaking in God's presence and knowing that He listens. How incredible! It is coming before the unseen ruler of this universe and acknowledging that He is. That He is awesome and more than worthy of our praises; that He is forgiving and willing to draw us back into personal relationship with Him by a work He has already completed through Jesus Christ; that He is powerful and able to do more than we can ask and imagine; and that He is loving and cares deeply about a little planet that spins through empty space with so many lonely creatures crawling across its surface. True prayer is humble. True prayer is not focused inward, but upward.

This book was compiled from the writings of wonderful servants of God who have discovered, in their own walk with Him, something of the marvels of prayer. It is a year's journey into the discovery of a deeper communion with God. What could be so magnificent? What could be so fulfilling? What could be so vital to each of us, no matter where we find ourselves today in our spiritual walk?

There is an attitude that has long plagued our human race that says we can get what we want from God if we follow the right procedures. Prayer is not a procedure. God will not measure your life of prayer by how you perform it, but by what is in your heart—by what attitude toward Him it exudes. He knows us, better than we know ourselves. And because of His deep love for us He rewards our reaching out to Him with great and amazing answers to our prayers. We can trust all of our hopes, dreams, and fears to the One "who is able to do immeasurably more than all we ask or imagine, according to his power that is at work within us" (Ephesians 3:20).

Neither does the Bible require us to grasp and claw to make our prayers become more effective. And that is a wonderful thing. Consider the contrast shown by the pagan priests who competed with Elijah in 1 Kings 18 to make their own false god burn up their sacrifice. They danced until they were exhausted, they cut their flesh and tore their clothes. All to no avail. What was it in Elijah's prayer that touched the very heart of heaven? His words were simple. "O Lord, God of Abraham, Isaac and Israel, let it be known today that you are God in Israel and that I am your servant and have done all these things at your command. Answer me, O Lord, answer me, so these people will know that you, O Lord, are God, and that you are turning their hearts back again."

Elijah prayed, in humility, that God would perform the great work that he knew was in God's heart—to turn the people back to Him. And fire fell from heaven. It is God's business to perform great works. Our part is to pray, as incense before the throne of God, ever pleasing Him and reminding Him that there are, yet, those of the human race who adore Him and are intent on serving Him. Prayer is not straining for answers. Prayer is resting in the promise that God will never leave us nor forsake us, that He is always working for our good.

My own prayer for this book is that God will use its message in your heart for whatever work He has planned this year: that He will use these words, from so many seasoned Christians, and the time you spend seeking Him in prayer to fan the flames of His Spirit in your heart so that you would be kindled to new awareness of this wonderful power of prayer, whether you have been praying for many years or are just beginning.

God bless you.

SUGGESTIONS FOR THE USE OF THIS JOURNAL

As with any journal, this is intended to be personal. We have, in arranging it, made as much provision as possible for a wide variety of journaling styles. Please allow me to make a few suggestions that you may find helpful.

1. The pages have purposely been left without division by days. This allows you to write as much as is in your heart one day or just what you are able the next. It also makes provision for those who choose to journal less than daily. By dating your sections near the margin, it should be easy to create for yourself an orderly and rewarding record of your prayers and thoughts.

2. The calendars for each month are not dated, but space has been left for you to do this using the yearly calendars printed in the front of the book. We have supplied these calendars, and lined spaces that follow them so that you may note birthdays, events, and occasions that need special prayer. You might even consider filling in requests topically; praying for missionaries one month, then local schools and teachers next. The possibilities are endless.

   These lists keep your requests close at hand when you begin praying and can become an excellent record of God's answers if you take a moment later to also record where you have seen Him work. One of the most wonderful experiences of journaling is going back over what you have written to see how His hand has touched your life and the lives of those you love.

3. There is space provided for a response to the monthly theme or a separate monthly goal that you have set for yourself. This keeps your personal focus before you as each month progresses.

4. Along the bottom of each page is a word study that deals with one area of the month's theme. There are enough to take two or three of these scriptures daily, perhaps even writing those that especially speak to your heart into the journal itself.

5. Finally, the format was designed to be followed month by month. If you are not starting your journaling in January, I suggest you begin journaling using the pages of the current month and continue through to December. Then go back to January for the new year and complete the earlier portion.

1995

January
S	M	T	W	T	F	S
1	2	3	4	5	6	7
8	9	10	11	12	13	14
15	16	17	18	19	20	21
22	23	24	25	26	27	28
29	30	31				

February
S	M	T	W	T	F	S
			1	2	3	4
5	6	7	8	9	10	11
12	13	14	15	16	17	18
19	20	21	22	23	24	25
26	27	28				

March
S	M	T	W	T	F	S
			1	2	3	4
5	6	7	8	9	10	11
12	13	14	15	16	17	18
19	20	21	22	23	24	25
26	27	28	29	30	31	

April
S	M	T	W	T	F
2	3	4	5	6	7
9	10	11	12	13	14
16	17	18	19	20	21
23	24	25	26	27	28
30					

May
S	M	T	W	T	F	S
	1	2	3	4	5	6
7	8	9	10	11	12	13
14	15	16	17	18	19	20
21	22	23	24	25	26	27
28	29	30	31			

June
S	M	T	W	T	F	S
				1	2	3
4	5	6	7	8	9	10
11	12	13	14	15	16	17
18	19	20	21	22	23	24
25	26	27	28	29	30	

July
S	M	T	W	T	F	S
						1
2	3	4	5	6	7	8
9	10	11	12	13	14	15
16	17	18	19	20	21	22
23	24	25	26	27	28	29
30	31					

August
S	M	T	W	T	F
	1	2	3	4
6	7	8	9	10	11
13	14	15	16	17	18
20	21	22	23	24	25
27	28	29	30	31	

September
S	M	T	W	T	F	S
					1	2
3	4	5	6	7	8	9
10	11	12	13	14	15	16
17	18	19	20	21	22	23
24	25	26	27	28	29	30

October
S	M	T	W	T	F	S
1	2	3	4	5	6	7
8	9	10	11	12	13	14
15	16	17	18	19	20	21
22	23	24	25	26	27	28
29	30	31				

November
S	M	T	W	T	F	S
			1	2	3	4
5	6	7	8	9	10	11
12	13	14	15	16	17	18
19	20	21	22	23	24	25
26	27	28	29	30		

December
S	M	T	W	T	F
					1
3	4	5	6	7	8
10	11	12	13	14	15
17	18	19	20	21	22
24	25	26	27	28	29
31					

1996

January
S	M	T	W	T	F	S
	1	2	3	4	5	6
7	8	9	10	11	12	13
14	15	16	17	18	19	20
21	22	23	24	25	26	27
28	29	30	31			

February
S	M	T	W	T	F	S
				1	2	3
4	5	6	7	8	9	10
11	12	13	14	15	16	17
18	19	20	21	22	23	24
25	26	27	28	29		

March
S	M	T	W	T	F	S
					1	2
3	4	5	6	7	8	9
10	11	12	13	14	15	16
17	18	19	20	21	22	23
24	25	26	27	28	29	30
31						

April
S	M	T	W	T	F	S
	1	2	3	4	5	6
7	8	9	10	11	12	13
14	15	16	17	18	19	20
21	22	23	24	25	26	27
28	29	30				

May
S	M	T	W	T	F	S
			1	2	3	4
5	6	7	8	9	10	11
12	13	14	15	16	17	18
19	20	21	22	23	24	25
26	27	28	29	30	31	

June
S	M	T	W	T	F	S
						1
2	3	4	5	6	7	8
9	10	11	12	13	14	15
16	17	18	19	20	21	22
23	24	25	26	27	28	29
30						

July
S	M	T	W	T	F	S
	1	2	3	4	5	6
7	8	9	10	11	12	13
14	15	16	17	18	19	20
21	22	23	24	25	26	27
28	29	30	31			

August
S	M	T	W	T	F
				1	2
4	5	6	7	8	9
11	12	13	14	15	16
18	19	20	21	22	23
25	26	27	28	29	30

September
S	M	T	W	T	F	S
1	2	3	4	5	6	7
8	9	10	11	12	13	14
15	16	17	18	19	20	21
22	23	24	25	26	27	28
29	30					

October
S	M	T	W	T	F	S
		1	2	3	4	5
6	7	8	9	10	11	12
13	14	15	16	17	18	19
20	21	22	23	24	25	26
27	28	30	31			

November
S	M	T	W	T	F	S
					1	2
3	4	5	6	7	8	9
10	11	12	13	14	15	16
17	18	19	20	21	22	23
24	25	26	27	28	29	30

December
S	M	T	W	T	F
1	2	3	4	5	6
8	9	10	11	12	13
15	16	17	18	19	20
22	23	24	25	26	27
29	30	31			

1997

January
S	M	T	W	T	F	S
			1	2	3	4
5	6	7	8	9	10	11
12	13	14	15	16	17	18
19	20	21	22	23	24	25
26	27	28	29	30	31	

February
S	M	T	W	T	F	S
						1
2	3	4	5	6	7	8
9	10	11	12	13	14	15
16	17	18	19	20	21	22
23	24	25	26	27	28	

March
S	M	T	W	T	F	S
						1
2	3	4	5	6	7	8
9	10	11	12	13	14	15
16	17	18	19	20	21	22
23	24	25	26	27	28	29
30	31					

April
S	M	T	W	T	F	S
		1	2	3	4	5
6	7	8	9	10	11	12
13	14	15	16	17	18	19
20	21	22	23	24	25	26
27	28	29	30			

May
S	M	T	W	T	F	S
				1	2	3
4	5	6	7	8	9	10
11	12	13	14	15	16	17
18	19	20	21	22	23	24
25	26	27	28	29	30	31

June
S	M	T	W	T	F	S
1	2	3	4	5	6	7
8	9	10	11	12	13	14
15	16	17	18	19	20	21
22	23	24	25	26	27	28
29	30					

July
S	M	T	W	T	F	S
		1	2	3	4	5
6	7	8	9	10	11	12
13	14	15	16	17	18	19
20	21	22	23	24	25	26
27	28	29	30	31		

August
S	M	T	W	T	F	S
					1	2
3	4	5	6	7	8	9
10	11	12	13	14	15	16
17	18	19	20	21	22	23
24	25	26	27	28	29	30
31						

September
S	M	T	W	T	F	S
	1	2	3	4	5	6
7	8	9	10	11	12	13
14	15	16	17	18	19	20
21	22	23	24	25	26	27
28	29	30				

October
S	M	T	W	T	F	S
			1	2	3	4
5	6	7	8	9	10	11
12	13	14	15	16	17	18
19	20	21	22	23	24	25
26	27	28	29	30	31	

November
S	M	T	W	T	F	S
						1
2	3	4	5	6	7	8
9	10	11	12	13	14	15
16	17	18	19	20	21	22
23	24	25	26	27	28	29
30						

December
S	M	T	W	T	F	S
	1	2	3	4	5	6
7	8	9	10	11	12	13
14	15	16	17	18	19	20
21	22	23	24	25	26	27
28	29	30	31			

1998

January
S	M	T	W	T	F	S
				1	2	3
4	5	6	7	8	9	10
11	12	13	14	15	16	17
18	19	20	21	22	23	24
25	26	27	28	29	30	31

February
S	M	T	W	T	F	S
1	2	3	4	5	6	7
8	9	10	11	12	13	14
15	16	17	18	19	20	21
22	23	24	25	26	27	28

March
S	M	T	W	T	F	S
1	2	3	4	5	6	7
8	9	10	11	12	13	14
15	16	17	18	19	20	21
22	23	24	25	26	27	28
29	30	31				

April
S	M	T	W	T	F	S
			1	2	3	4
5	6	7	8	9	10	11
12	13	14	15	16	17	18
19	20	21	22	23	24	25
26	27	28	29	30		

May
S	M	T	W	T	F	S
					1	2
3	4	5	6	7	8	9
10	11	12	13	14	15	16
17	18	19	20	21	22	23
24	25	26	27	28	29	30
31						

June
S	M	T	W	T	F	S
	1	2	3	4	5	6
7	8	9	10	11	12	13
14	15	16	17	18	19	20
21	22	23	24	25	26	27
28	29	30				

July
S	M	T	W	T	F	S
			1	2	3	4
5	6	7	8	9	10	11
12	13	14	15	16	17	18
19	20	21	22	23	24	25
26	27	28	29	30	31	

August
S	M	T	W	T	F	S
						1
2	3	4	5	6	7	8
9	10	11	12	13	14	15
16	17	18	19	20	21	22
23	24	25	26	27	28	29
30	31					

September
S	M	T	W	T	F	S
		1	2	3	4	5
6	7	8	9	10	11	12
13	14	15	16	17	18	19
20	21	22	23	24	25	26
27	28	29	30			

October
S	M	T	W	T	F	S
				1	2	3
4	5	6	7	8	9	10
11	12	13	14	15	16	17
18	19	20	21	22	23	24
25	26	27	28	29	30	31

November
S	M	T	W	T	F	S
1	2	3	4	5	6	7
8	9	10	11	12	13	14
15	16	17	18	19	20	21
22	23	24	25	26	27	28
29	30					

December
S	M	T	W	T	F	S
		1	2	3	4	5
6	7	8	9	10	11	12
13	14	15	16	17	18	19
20	21	22	23	24	25	26
27	28	29	30	31		

January

19_____

SUN	MON	TUES	WED	THURS	FRI	SAT

I cannot pray in the name of Jesus to have my own will; the name of Jesus is not a signature of no importance, but the decisive factor in prayer. The fact that the name of Jesus is invoked does not mean that a prayer really is in the name of Jesus. But it means I must pray in such a manner that I dare name Jesus in my prayer, that is to say, think of Him, think His Holy Will together with what I am praying.
—Soren Kierkegaard, 1813-1855, Danish philosopher and author

Occasions for special prayer.

Ongoing prayer concerns.

By Jesus' very example, we know that praise is the first essential element in prayer. When we turn our focus away from ourselves and our lives, we enter God's presence in a very dramatic way. Praise becomes a preparation of our hearts to begin this conversation with our God, the Creator of the universe, and Savior of mankind. We must always remember to focus on the Person to whom we speak, and our position in that relationship. When we become fully aware of the great chasm that God crossed to reach us and how completely He draws us into His amazing love without reservation or condemnation, we find our prayers have changed—as does our outlook on life, even during hardships. Consider these words written by Joni Eareckson Tada, who has learned firsthand to praise God, courageously, in time of trouble. Through the sweet spirit which God has nurtured in her even through paralysis in her youth, her life and writings are an inspiration to so many of us.

"If you praise the Lord through a minor hardship or a major trial, you are offering a sacrifice of praise. Such a sacrifice costs you plenty—your pride, your anger, your human logic, and the luxury of your complaining tongue. A sacrifice of praise costs you your will, your resentment, and even your desire to have your own way in a situation. And for whose sake do we give up these things? We do so for the sake of Christ and for His glory."

"Whether it's a financial crunch, a sudden illness, or a personal defeat, if you fix your heart on praise to God, then you have offered a sacrifice. If you've ever cried during those heartbreaking difficulties, 'Lord, I will hope in You and praise You more and more,' then you know you have offered words which have cost you plenty. Praise in those circumstances is painful. Nevertheless, it is logical, even if our logic argues that God has no idea what He's doing."

Joni Eareckson Tada, A *Quiet Place in a Crazy World*
Multnomah Books, Questar Publishers, 1993

By developing the habit of beginning prayer with praise, your prayer life becomes enhanced and focused. This month, perhaps you would like to explore your own praise relationship with God.

❧

Personal response/goal:

_____

_____

_____

_____

_____

WORSHIP

Prepare my heart, Lord, to receive afresh the King of Kings. Purge me with Your Holy Spirit that He may find a clean, warm, and responsive abode in me. Help me to face the new year with courage, enthusiasm, and faith.

—Catherine Marshall and
   Leonard LeSourd,
   My Personal Prayer Diary,
   Chosen Books, 1979

POWERFUL: Exodus 15:1-21   Deuteronomy 8:17-18   2 Chronicles 20:6   Job 9:1-12
Psalm 77:11-20   Jeremiah 10:12-16   Jude 24-25

WORSHIP

Come and listen, all you who fear God; let me tell you what he has done for me.

I cried out to him with my mouth; his praise was on my tongue.

If I had cherished sin in my heart, the Lord would not have listened; but God has surely listened and heard my voice in prayer.

Praise be to God, who has not rejected my prayer or withheld his love from me!

Psalm 66:16-20

APPROACHABLE: Deuteronomy 4:29   Deuteronomy 30:11-14   2 Chronicles 7:11-15
Psalm 65:1-4   Romans 10:5-13   Ephesians 3:10-12   Hebrews 4:14-16

January

W O R S H I P

I am confounded to think that God, who hath done so much for me, should have so little from me. But this is my comfort, when I come into heaven, I shall understand perfectly what He hath done for me, and then shall I be able to praise Him as I ought.

— Anne Bradstreet,
  1612-1672, poet

✿

ETERNAL: Psalm 90:1-12   Psalm 93   Psalm 119:89-91   Ecclesiastes 3:11-14
Isaiah 26:3-4   Isaiah 40:27-31   Hebrews 1:10-12

January

WORSHIP

Come and see the works
of the Lord, the desolations
he has brought on the
earth.

He makes wars cease to
the ends of the earth; he
breaks the bow and shat-
ters the spear, he burns the
shields with fire.

Be still, and know that I
am God; I will be exalted
among the nations, I will
be exalted in the earth.

Psalm 46:8-10

AWESOME: Exodus 34:10   Job 25:2   Psalm 47   Psalm 66:1-7   Ecclesiastes 5:7
Zephaniah 2:10-11   Hebrews 12:28-29

January

WORSHIP

As for God, his way is
perfect; the word of the
Lord is flawless.

He is a shield for all
who take refuge in him.

For who is God besides
the Lord?

And who is the Rock
except our God?

It is God who arms me
with strength and makes
my way perfect.

He makes my feet like
the feet of a deer; he
enables me to stand on the
heights.

Psalm 18:30-33

PERFECT: Psalm 19:7-11   Psalm 119:96   Isaiah 25:1   Matthew 5:48
1 Corinthians 13:9-12   2 Corinthians 12:9   Hebrews 12:1-3

O God, whose throne is
heaven, whose footstool is
the earth below, whose
arms enlace the firmament,
nothing is hidden from Thy
sight: in the fastness of the
rock Thou see'st the dia-
mond, in the bottomless pit
of hell, Thou see'st Thine
own just judgment, in the
deep recesses of the human
heart, Thou see'st every
secret thought. O God,
my Savior, I turn to Thee.

— Margaret of Navarre,
    1492-1549

JUST: Deuteronomy 32:3-4   Nehemiah 9:32-33   Psalm 33:1-5   Isaiah 30:15-18
Zephaniah 3:5   Romans 2:6-11   I Peter 1:17-22

Thou didst break the flaming sword and didst restore to paradise the man that was crucified with Thee and implored Thy mercy. Remember me, too, in Thy kingdom; because I, too, was crucified with Thee, having nailed my flesh to the cross for fear of Thee. And of Thy judgments have I been afraid. Let not the terrible chasm separate me from Thy elect. Nor let the slanderer stand against me in the way; nor let my sin be found before Thine eyes, if in anything I have sinned in word or deed or thought, or been led astray by the weakness of our nature.

O Thou who hast power on earth to forgive sins, forgive me, that I may be refreshed and may be found before Thee when I put off my body, without defilement on my soul. But may my soul be received into Thy Hands spotless and undefiled, as an offering before Thee.

—Macrina, 327-379,
   devoted early Christian
   on her deathbed

FORGIVING: Numbers 14:17-19   Psalm 19:12-13   Psalm 130   Daniel 9:17-19
            Micah 7:18-19   Hebrews 9:19-28   1 John 1:8-10

WORSHIP

I wondered over again for the hundredth time what could be the principle which, in the wildest, most lawless, fantastically chaotic, apparently capricious work of nature, always kept it beautiful. The beauty of holiness must be at the heart of it somehow, I thought. Because our God is so free from stain, so loving, so unselfish, so good, so altogether what He wants us to be, so holy, therefore all His works declare Him in beauty; His fingers can touch nothing but to mould it into loveliness; and even the play of His elements is in grace and tenderness of form.

—George MacDonald, 1824-1905, Scottish author

CREATIVE: Psalm 8   Psalm 104   Psalm 139   Isaiah 45:2-8   Isaiah 45:18-19
Amos 4:13   Ephesians 2:10

O sweet and loving God,
When I stay asleep too long,
Oblivious to all Your many
blessings,
   Then, please, wake me up,
   And sing to me Your
joyful song.
   It is a song without
noise or notes.
   It is a song of love beyond
words, Of faith beyond the
power of human telling.
   I can hear it in my soul,
When You awaken me to
Your presence.

—Mechthild of Magdeburg,
   ca. 1210-1280

FAITHFUL: Exodus 34:1-7   Deuteronomy 7:9   Psalm 18:25-28   Psalm 111
Psalm 145:13-21   Lamentations 3:22-24   1 Corinthians 10:13

January

WORSHIP

The voice of the Lord is over the waters…

The voice of the Lord is powerful; The voice of the Lord is majestic…

The voice of the Lord strikes with flashes of lightning.

The voice of the Lord shakes the desert…

Psalm 29:3-8,
selected portions

Lord, Your very voice is awesome. I am amazed by it. And in your creative inspiration You have blessed me with a voice, as well. Please guide my use of it. Help me understand that I can build up or tear down and destroy. What incredible, frightening power You have given me with my voice.

HOLY: Psalm 96:1-9   Psalm 99   Proverbs 9:10   Isaiah 8:13-17   Hebrews 12:10
Revelation 4:1-8   Revelation 15:1-4

We should be careful
in our thinking, as well as
in our conversation, to
remember that we are
responsible for the attitude
of the next generation—
to remember that our
carelessness is affecting this
next generation, and we
have responsibility.

"One generation shall
praise thy works to another,
and shall declare thy mighty
acts...They shall abundantly
utter the memory of thy
great goodness, and shall
sing of thy righteousness.
The Lord is gracious, and
full of compassion; slow to
anger, and of great mercy...
The Lord is righteous in all
his ways, and holy in all his
works. The Lord is nigh
unto all them that call upon
him, to all that call upon
him in truth."

Psalm 145:4, 7-8, 17-18,
KJV emphasis added

—Edith Schaeffer, *A Way of
Seeing*, Fleming H. Revell
Publishing, 1977

MERCIFUL: Deuteronomy 4:31   Nehemiah 9:19-21   Psalm 25:4-15   Psalm 103:8-14
Joel 2:13   Jonah 3   Titus 3:3-7

January

We look upon prayer as a means of getting things for ourselves; the Bible idea of prayer is that we may get to know God himself.

—Oswald Chambers,
  My Utmost for His Highest,
  used by permission of
  Discovery House
  Publishers, 1663

❀

FATHERLY: Isaiah 63:15-16 Matthew 6:5-15 Matthew 7:7-11 John 16:23-28
John 17:24-26 James 1:17 1 John 3:1-3

FEBRUARY

19_____

SUN	MON	TUES	WED	THURS	FRI	SAT

He who prays little will pray less, but he who prays much will pray more.
— *Charles Spurgeon, English preacher 1834-1892*

Occasions for special prayer.

_____
_____
_____
_____
_____
_____
_____

Ongoing prayer concerns.

_____
_____
_____
_____
_____
_____
_____

The Love of God

BY EDITH SCHAEFFER

Over and over again one hears people say, "I can't believe in a God who would have only one way to approach Him. What about the heathen nations? What about other religions and philosophies? God cannot be a loving God or a compassionate God, if He allows people to be lost." Yes, unbelievers use this as an excuse not to come to God—the fact that they believe they have within their own minds and hearts a more compassionate and loving attitude, feeling, and action toward the people of history than God does... It is a titanic thing to think of the lack of awe and fear on the part of a finite, minuscule creature—with a span of background which could not be more than one century of his own lifetime—presuming to judge the Eternal God so lightly and easily, rather than seeking to discover something of the marvel of the love of God, the wonder of His compassion—compassion not for friends but for enemies. Natural man is at enmity against God. That is, man is really an enemy of God before he becomes a child of God through what Jesus the Lamb did for him in taking his punishment. The love of God is such that the Second Person of the Trinity died for enemies! This is a love which man cannot fathom.

However, it is not just those who are non-Christians, atheists, or people caught in false religions who set themselves up to judge the compassion and love of God. Christians often slip into thinking and feeling that they have more love, more compassion...than God. Perhaps Christians don't put this into a clear outline in their own minds and feelings. But in conversation, that which is in the wells of their hearts comes out in the buckets of their verbalized questions and doubts....

God has given us access to Him through communication. We are not allowed to criticize, but to come asking, pleading, interceding for others. We are given the possibility of affecting the history of others through our prayer and our willingness to be involved. Rather than simply weeping, we should weep and pray, asking that God would use us in some very real way in this moment of history.

Second, we should recognize that our "feelings" should give us compassion towards God. If we suffer because of other people's suffering, we can understand in a small way how Jesus cried, "O Jerusalem, Jerusalem...how oft would I have gathered you under my wings as a mother hen her chickens, but ye would not!" (See Matthew 23:37).

Edith Schaeffer, *A Way of Seeing*, Fleming H. Revell Publishing, 1977

❧

Personal response/goal:

_____

_____

_____

_____

*Almighty God, I have found
that to know Thee only as
a philosopher; to have the
most sublime and curious
speculations concerning Thine
essence, Thine attributes,
Thy providence; to be able to
demonstrate Thy being from
all or any of the works of
nature and to discourse with
the greatest elegancy and
propriety of words of Thine
existence or operations, will
avail me nothing, unless at
the same time I know Thee
experimentally: unless my
heart perceive and know Thee
to be its supreme good, its only
happiness; unless my soul feel
and acknowledge that she can
find no repose, no peace, no
joy, but in loving and being
beloved by Thee; and does
accordingly rest in Thee as
the center of her being, the
fountain of her pleasure,
the origin of all virtue and
goodness, her light, her life,
her strength, her all; everything
she wants or wishes in this
world and forever.*

—Susanna Wesley, 1669-1742,
mother of John and Charles
Wesley

❀

HEART: 1 Samuel 16:7   Psalm 51:10-12   Proverbs 21:1-2   Jeremiah 17:9-10
Ezekiel 11:19-20   2 Corinthians 4:6   1 Thessalonians 3:13

Behold, Lord, an empty vessel that needs to be filled. My Lord, fill it. I am weak in the faith; strengthen me. I am cold in love; warm me and make me fervent that my love may go out to my neighbor. I do not have a strong and firm faith; at times I doubt and am unable to trust You altogether. O Lord, help me. Strengthen my faith and trust in You. In You I have sealed the treasures of all I have. I am poor; You are rich and came to be merciful to the poor. I am a sinner; You are upright. With me there is an abundance of sin; in You is the fulness of righteousness. Therefore I will remain with You of whom I can receive but to whom I may not give. Amen.

—Martin Luther,
   1483-1546, German
   religious reformer

HUMAN LOVE: Genesis 29:32-34   Judges 16:15-16   2 Samuel 13:1-2   2 Samuel 19:1-7
                       Job 19:13-22   Matthew 22:34-40   1 John 3:11-24

THE *February* LOVE OF GOD

Beware of any work for God which enables you to evade concentration on Him. A great many Christian workers worship their work.

—Oswald Chambers, My *Utmost for His Highest*, used by permission of Discovery House Publishers, 1963

❧

GOD'S LOVE: Isaiah 63:8-9   Jeremiah 31:3   Zephaniah 3:17   John 3:16-18
Romans 8:35-39   Ephesians 3:14-21   1 John 4:7-21

THE *February* OF GOD

We love our children for who they are now and for each and every wonderful thing they have done in the past. God, as our Father, loves us for all these things, but He also has the incredible ability to love us for all the things He knows we will be. As you stand before Him, He sees in you what you will become by His strength. He loves you for that as well.

❧

CHOSEN: Deuteronomy 10:14-15   Isaiah 41:9-10   John 15:16   Romans 8:28-30
Ephesians 1:3-6   Ephesians 2:4-10   2 Thessalonians 2:13-17

THE *February* GOD

*In your unfailing love
you will lead the people
you have redeemed.*

*In your strength you
will guide them to your
holy dwelling…*

*You will bring them
in and plant them on
the mountain of your
inheritance — the place,
O Lord, you made for
your dwelling, the
sanctuary, O Lord,
your hands established.*

Exodus 15:13, 17

REDEMPTION: Psalm 49:7-9   Psalm 130:7-8   Luke 1:68-75   Romans 3:21-31
Colossians 1:13-14   I Peter 1:18-20   Revelation 5:9-10

THE LOVE OF GOD

February

Infinite Love will never give a stone when bread is asked for, or a scorpion in place of an egg. But what will Infinite Love give if our prayer is for a scorpion?

—Elisabeth Elliot, *Love Has a Price Tag*, Christian Herald Books, 1979

❦

BLESSING: Genesis 12:2-3   Genesis 26:3-5   Genesis 28:13-15   Deuteronomy 28:1-14
Psalm 72:17   Acts 3:17-26   Galatians 3:6-14

THE *February* OF GOD

Take every dream within your heart
To God who really cares;
He longs to hold you in His Arms,
He listens for your prayers.

Take every sigh and every tear
To Him who understands.
Exchange these things for lasting peace
Within His loving Hands.

—Audrey McDaniel, *Love's Promise*,
C. R. Gibson Company, 1973

UNDERSTANDING: 1 Chronicles 28:9   Psalm 147:5, 10-11   Isaiah 11:1-5
Isaiah 40:28   Jeremiah 10:12   Matthew 6:25-33   1 Peter 5:6-7

THE *February* LOVE OF GOD

Father,
I am seeking:
I am hesitant and uncertain,
but will You, O God, watch over
each step of mine and guide me.

—Augustine, 354-430, early
   philosopher and religious leader

GUIDE: Exodus 13:21-22   Psalm 23   Psalm 25:4-5   Psalm 136   Isaiah 58:11
2 Corinthians 2:14   Revelation 7:17

THE *February* OF GOD

*My secret is quite
simple: I pray.*

—Mother Teresa

❧

SERVITUDE: Deuteronomy 10:12-13   Joshua 24:15, 24   Matthew 20:26-28
Luke 12:35-37   John 12:25-26   Romans 14:15-18   2 Corinthians 9:10-15

THE *February* OF GOD

*I can hardly claim
to belong to God as
long as my own desires
and ambitions are
considered above His.*

—Janette Oke

❧

SUBMISSION: Matthew 6:10   Matthew 26:36-42   Acts 18:21   Colossians 1:9
Hebrews 12:7-10   James 3:17   James 4:7-8

THE *February* GOD

My prayer is not for them alone. I pray also for those who will believe in me through their message, that all of them may be one, Father, just as you are in me and I am in you. May they also be in us so that the world may believe that you have sent me. I have given them the glory that you gave me, that they may be one as we are one: I in them and you in me. May they be brought to complete unity to let the world know that you sent me and have loved them even as you have loved me.

John 17:20-23

❈

UNITY: John 15:1-17   Romans 12:4-8   1 Corinthians 1:10   1 Corinthians 12:12-27
Ephesians 2:11-22   Ephesians 4:1-6   Colossians 3:12-17

THE *February* LOVE OF GOD

...Christ loved the church and gave himself up for her to make her holy, cleansing her by the washing with water through the word, and to present her to himself as a radiant church, without stain or wrinkle or any other blemish, but holy and blameless.

Ephesians 5:25b-27

❧

CHURCH: Matthew 16:13-18   Colossians 1:15-20   Revelation 2:7, 11, 17
Revelation 2:26-29   Revelation 3:1-6   Revelation 3:19-22   Revelation 22:12-16

March

SUN	MON	TUES	WED	THURS	FRI	SAT

Forgiveness is the fragrance the violet sheds on the heel that has crushed it.
—Mark Twain, 1835-1910, American author

Occasions for special prayer.

Ongoing prayer concerns.

Forgiveness

BY CORRIE TEN BOOM

One day I saw a lady in a meeting who did not look into my eyes. Suddenly I recognized her. She was a nurse who had been very cruel to my dying sister when we were in Ravensbruck Concentration Camp during the war. When I saw her, a feeling of bitterness, almost hatred, came into my heart. How my dying sister had suffered because of her! The moment I felt that hatred in my heart, I knew that I myself had no forgiveness. It was the Lord Jesus who said to us: "If ye forgive not men their trespasses, neither will your Father forgive your trespasses."

I knew I had to forgive her, but I could not. Then I had a good talk with the Lord about it when I was at home later. "Lord, You know I cannot forgive her. My sister suffered too much because of her cruelties. I know, Lord, that I must forgive, but I cannot." Then the Lord gave me: "The love of God is shed abroad in our hearts by the Holy Ghost which is given unto us" Romans 5:5, KJV.

The Lord taught me a prayer: "Thank You, Lord, for Romans 5:5. Thank You, Jesus, that You brought into my heart God's love by the Holy Spirit who is given to me. Thank You, Father, that Your love in me is stronger than my hatred and bitterness." The same moment I knew I could forgive.

I told a friend about my experience and she said, "Oh, I know that nurse. She works in a hospital not far from here."

"Can you call her?"

"Sure I can." She called the nurse and I had a talk with her over the telephone, telling her that when I had the next meeting that evening, I would have a different message and would very much like her to come.

Her answer was, "You would like to see me in your meeting?"

"Yes, that is why I phoned. I should like it very much."

"Then I will come." She did come, and during the entire evening she looked into my eyes while I spoke. After the meeting, I had a talk with her. I told her that I had been bitter, but that God's Holy Spirit in me had brought His love instead of hatred and that now I loved her. I told her that it was through Jesus Christ who bore our sins on the cross. He forgave us, but He also fills our hearts with God's love through the Holy Spirit, and that is why I could invite her to come to the second meeting.

I told her more and at the end of our talk that nurse accepted the Lord Jesus Christ as her personal Savior and Lord. Do you see the miracle? I, who had hated her, was used by God to bring her to the acceptance of Jesus Christ. Not only will the Lord cleanse us by His blood but He will also use us....

Yes, we never touch the ocean of God's love so much as when we love our enemies. It is a joy to accept forgiveness, but it is almost a greater joy to give forgiveness.

Corrie ten Boom, *He Cares, He Comforts*, Fleming H. Revell Publishing, 1977

Personal response/goal:

Whatever weakens your reason, impairs the tenderness of your conscience, obscures your sense of God, or takes away the relish of spiritual things; in short, whatever increases the strength and authority of your body over your mind—that thing is sin to you.

—Susanna Wesley, 1669-1742, mother of John and Charles Wesley

SIN: Genesis 4:6-7   Psalm 14:1-3   Psalm 51:5   Ezekiel 18:20-23   Matthew 15:18-20
Romans 7:7-25   Romans 8:1-17

March

It may be easier to understand what forgiveness is, if we first clear away misconceptions about what it does. It does not wipe out the consequences of the sin. The words and images used for forgiveness in the New Testament frequently have to do with the cancellation of a debt: and it is scarcely necessary to point out that when a debt is canceled, this does not mean that the money is miraculously restored from nowhere...in every case the consequences are borne by somebody.

—Dorothy L. Sayers,
   Unpopular Opinions,
   Harcourt Brace and
   Company, 1947

SACRIFICE: Genesis 8:20-22   Genesis 22:1-14   Leviticus 1:1-17   Job 1:5
Isaiah 1:11-18   Hebrews 9:1-10   Hebrews 10:1-18

March

F O R G I V E N E S S

Only as we bow in contrition, confession, and repentance at the foot of the Cross, can we find forgiveness. There is the grace of God! We don't deserve it! A man said some time ago, "When I get to the judgment of God, all that I will ask for is justice." My beloved friend, if you get justice, then you will go to hell. You don't want justice. What you want is mercy.

—Billy Graham,
   The Hour of Decision, 1967

❧

MERCY: Genesis 8:1   Nehemiah 9:31   Jeremiah 3:12-13   Luke 23:39-43
Romans 9:15-16   Romans 10:8-11   James 2:12-13

March

FORGIVENESS

My dear children, I write this to you so that you will not sin. But if anybody does sin, we have one who speaks to the Father in our defense— Jesus Christ, the Righteous One. He is the atoning sacrifice for our sins, and not only for ours but also for the sins of the whole world.

1 John 2:1-2

CONFESSION: Numbers 5:6-7   Nehemiah 9:1-3   Psalm 38:18   Proverbs 28:13
Daniel 9:4-5   Luke 5:8-9   1 John 1:9

To do it no more is the truest repentance.

—Martin Luther,
   1483-1546, German
   religious reformer

❀

REPENTANCE: Ezekiel 18:30-32   Matthew 3:11-12   Mark 1:14-15   Luke 24:46-49
Acts 17:30-31   2 Corinthians 7:10-11   2 Peter 3:9

FORGIVENESS

Sin, whether committed by us or committed against us, mars and scars the image of God. Restoration to that beautiful image of Christlikeness comes as we are transformed by the Word of God. I have seen it in my life, and in the lives of countless others.

—Kay Arthur,
  Lord, Heal My Hurts,
  Harvest House, 1989

RESTORATION: Deuteronomy 30:1-3 Psalm 80:3 Psalm 126:4-6 Isaiah 49:6
Zephaniah 3:20 Zechariah 10:6 1 Peter 5:10-11

*O Lord, do not rebuke me
in your anger or discipline me
in your wrath.*

*Be merciful to me, Lord,
for I am faint;*

*O Lord, heal me, for my
bones are in agony.*

*The Lord has heard my
cry for mercy; the Lord
accepts my prayer.*

Psalm 6:1-2, 9

❧

HEALING: Deuteronomy 32:39   2 Chronicles 7:13-15   Job 5:17-18   Psalm 41:4
Psalm 107:19-21   Hosea 6:1   Revelation 22:1-5

F O R G I *March* V E N E S S

Master, they say that
when I seem
To be in speech with You,
   Since You make no replies,
it's all a dream—
   One talker aping two.

   They are half right, but not
as they Imagine; rather I
   Seek in myself the things
I meant to say,
   And lo! the wells are dry.

   Then, seeing me empty,
You forsake
   The Listener's role, and
through
   My dead lips breathe and
into utterance wake
   The thoughts I never knew.

—Excerpt "Prayer" by
  C.S. Lewis from *Poems by
  C.S. Lewis*, Harcourt Brace
  and Company, 1964

❀

COMMUNION: Exodus 33:7-11   1 Samuel 3:8-10   Job 29:2-4   Psalm 5:3   Psalm 16:7
2 Corinthians 5:17-21   Philippians 2:1-2

March

F O R G I V E N E S S

*Ask the sea if it will ever
want water? Do you not
know that the mercies of
God are inexhaustible?*

—Madame de Combe,
1656-1692

❧

FORGOTTEN: Psalm 32:1   Psalm 103:11-12   Isaiah 43:25   Isaiah 44:21-23
Jeremiah 31:34   Micah 7:18-19   2 Peter 1:5-9

FORGIVENESS

I have hidden your word in my heart that I might not sin against you.

Psalm 119:11

Let me not only hide your Word in my mind, make it burrow into my heart, Lord, and change who I am.

❋

GOD'S WORD: 2 Samuel 7:28   Isaiah 55:10-11   Ephesians 6:10-18   2 Timothy 2:15
2 Timothy 3:14, 17   Hebrews 4:12   1 Peter 1:23

March

F O R G I V E N E S S

Surely the arm of the Lord is not too short to save, nor his ear too dull to hear.

But your iniquities have separated you from your God; your sins have hidden his face from you, so that he will not hear.

Isaiah 59:1-2

SALVATION: Exodus 14:13   2 Chronicles 20:17   Esther 4:12-14   Joel 2:32
Romans 13:11-13   Ephesians 1:13-14   Philippians 1:19-24

March

F O R G I V E N E S S

Above all, love each other deeply, because love covers over a multitude of sins.

1 Peter 4:8

❀

KEPT FROM SIN: Genesis 20:6   Exodus 20:18-21   Psalm 4:4   Psalm 39:1
Proverbs 6:23-24   Matthew 6:14-15   Jude 24

SUN	MON	TUES	WED	THURS	FRI	SAT

Lord, teach us to understand that Your Son died to save us not from suffering but from ourselves, not from injustice, far less from justice, but from being unjust. He died that we might live—but live as He lives, by dying as He died, who died to himself.

—George MacDonald, 1824-1905, Scottish author

Occasions for special prayer.　　　　*Ongoing prayer concerns.*

_____　　　_____

_____　　　_____

_____　　　_____

_____　　　_____

_____　　　_____

_____　　　_____

_____　　　_____

_____　　　_____

Our Savior

They mocked and railed on Him and smote Him, they scourged and crucified Him. Well, they were people very remote from ourselves, and no doubt it was all done in the noblest and most beautiful manner. We should not like to think otherwise.

Unhappily, if we think about it at all, we must think otherwise. God was executed by people painfully like us, in a society very similar to our own—in the over-ripeness of the most splendid and sophisticated Empire the world has ever seen. In a nation famous for its religious genius and under a government renowned for its efficiency, He was executed by a corrupt church, a timid politician, and a fickle proletariat led by professional agitators. His executioners made vulgar jokes about Him, called Him filthy names, taunted Him, smacked Him in the face, flogged Him with the cat-o'-nine-tails, and hanged Him on the common gibbet—a bloody, dusty, sweaty, and sordid business.

If you show people that, they are shocked. So they should be. If that does not shock them, nothing can. If the mere representation of it has an air of irreverence, what is to be said about the deed? It is curious that people who are filled with horrified indignation whenever a cat kills a sparrow can hear that story of the killing of God told Sunday after Sunday and not experience any shock at all.

Dorothy L. Sayers, *The Man Born to Be King*, 1943

❧

Personal response/goal:

_____

_____

_____

_____

_____

_____

_____

_____

_____

_____

_____

_____

_____

_____

_____

_____

*He grew up before him
like a tender shoot, and like
a root out of dry ground.*

*He had no beauty or
majesty to attract us to him,
nothing in his appearance
that we should desire him.*

*He was despised and
rejected by men, a man of
sorrows, and familiar with
suffering.*

*Like one from whom men
hide their faces he was
despised, and we esteemed
him not....*

*But he was pierced for our
transgressions, he was
crushed for our iniquities; the
punishment that brought us
peace was upon him, and by
his wounds we are healed.*

*We all, like sheep, have
gone astray, each of us has
turned to his own way; and
the Lord has laid on him the
iniquity of us all.*

Isaiah 53:2-3, 5-6

PROPHECY: Deuteronomy 18:15   Psalm 22:14-19   Psalm 69:20-21   Isaiah 7:14
Isaiah 35:4-6   Isaiah 42:1-4   Zechariah 3:8-9

O U R   *April*   O R

Christ was never in a hurry. There was no rushing forward, no anticipating, no fretting over what might be. Each day's duties were done as every day brought them, and the rest was left with God.

—Mary Slessor,
  1848-1915, missionary

❧

MINISTRY: Matthew 5:17-18 Matthew 11:2-6 Luke 19:5-10 John 6:38-40
John 8:31-59 John 10:10, 22-28 Hebrews 2:14-15

OUR SAVIOR

When I survey the wondrous Cross
On which the Prince of Glory died,
My richest gain I count but loss,
And pour contempt on all my pride.

See, from His head, His hands, His feet,
Sorrow and love flow mingled down.
Did e'er such love and sorrow meet,
Or thorns compose so rich a crown?

Were the whole realm of nature mine,
That were a present far too small.
Love so amazing, so divine,
Demands my soul, my life, my all.

—Isaac Watts,
  from the hymn *When I Survey*

CROSS: Matthew 10:37-38   Matthew 27:3-5   Matthew 27:22-23, 32   John 19:19-22
John 19:25   Acts 2:22-24   1 Corinthians 1:18   Galatians 6:14

OUR *April* SAVIOR

There are three little men that live down inside of every one of us. One is intellect, another is emotion, and the third is will. Intellectually, you may accept Christ.

Emotionally, you may feel that you can love Him. However, until you have surrendered to Christ by a definite act of your will, you are not a Christian.

—Billy Graham, *The Hour of Decision*, 1958

SURRENDER: Matthew 4:18-20   Matthew 14:22-32   Matthew 16:13-23
Matthew 26:69-75   John 20:3–21:19   Acts 1:12–2:40   Acts 4:13

His aging face was rugged
and deeply lined, this head of
Wheaton's Bible department.
He may not have been the
best of teachers, Dr. H. C.
Thiessen, but he was one of
the godliest and kindest. My
mind frequently wandered as
he taught us from the textbook
on Bible doctrine which he
himself had written. But
when he came to the part
about God's Son giving
His life to redeem us sinful
mortals, the strong voice never
broke, but the tears would
begin to trickle down those
worn seams—as if they had
done it before, as if perhaps
they had sort of worn those
grooves there in the first place.

—Ruth Bell Graham,
    It's My Turn, Fleming H.
    Revell Publishing, 1982

GRATEFULNESS: Romans 6:17-18   Romans 7:24–8:2   1 Corinthians 11:23-28
2 Corinthians 4:13-15   2 Corinthians 9:15   Ephesians 5:15-20   Philippians 4:4-9

OUR *April* SAVIOR

*O Lord, grant me the
satisfaction of pleasing You;
not in work for You primarily,
but in relationship with You.
I would be like the woman
[who anointed Your feet with
expensive perfume] spending
herself totally, wastefully,
on Your behalf. Cause my
single-minded goal to be that
of satisfying You first. Then
will my longing heart be
satisfied in a love relationship
with You.*

—Catherine Marshall and
Leonard LeSourd, *My
Personal Prayer Diary*,
Chosen Books, 1979

❧

ANOINTED: Psalm 2:1-12   Psalm 89:50-51   Luke 4:16-21   John 1:32-34
John 12:1-8   Acts 10:34-43   2 Corinthians 1:18-22

I was free; but there was no one to welcome me to the land of freedom. I was a stranger in a strange land, and my home after all was down in the old cabin quarter, with the old folks, and my brothers and sisters. But to this solemn resolution I came; I was free, and they should be free also; I would make a home for them in the North, and the Lord helping me, I would bring them all there. Oh, how I prayed then, lying all alone on the cold, damp ground: "Oh, dear Lord," I said, "I ain't got no friend but You. Come to my help, Lord, for I'm in trouble!"

—Harriet Tubman, 1818-1913, leader in the Underground Railroad during the U.S. Civil War

FRIEND: Exodus 33:11   2 Chronicles 20:7   Job 16:19-21   Proverbs 27:6
Ecclesiastes 4:10   Matthew 11:19   Matthew 26:47-50

Gentle Shepherd, You have waited so long for me to turn to You. You have watched my wanderings, have even whispered warnings that I chose to ignore. And now, I come to You, having finally realized that You were what I needed all along. That You have always known the way for me to find happiness, and the path in which I should walk. And yet, You remain so gentle. You do not scold, You do not rebuke my contrite heart. And in Your whisper I feel the love that You have tried to express to me so often, while I have kept distance between us and looked elsewhere for someone to just love me, completely. Gentle Shepherd, teach me to follow you, anywhere.

SHEPHERD: Psalm 23   Isaiah 40:11   Zechariah 13:7   Matthew 26:31   John 10:11-13
Matthew 25:31-46   Hebrews 13:20-21

Make me sensible of real answers
to actual requests, as evidence of an
interchange between myself on earth
and my Savior in heaven.

—Thomas Chalmers, 1780-1847,
  Scottish minister and author

❋

SELF: Deuteronomy 9:6   Proverbs 16:18   Isaiah 64:6   Jeremiah 44:15-23
           Matthew 16:24   Romans 12:1-2   2 Corinthians 13:5

OUR *April* SAVIOR

It is a pleasant thing to behold the light, but sore eyes are not able to look upon it; the pure in heart shall see God, but the defiled in conscience shall rather choose to be buried under rocks and mountains than to behold the presence of the Lamb.

—Anne Bradstreet,
   1612-1672, American
   colonial poet

❧

RETURN: Matthew 24:12-14   Matthew 24:30-42   John 14:1-6   1 Corinthians 15:24-25
Colossians 3:1-4   1 Thessalonians 5:1-3   2 Peter 3:11-13

OUR *April* SAVIOR

*Here, before my eyes, is
my God and my King, the
mild and merciful Jesus,
crowned with sharp thorns;
shall I, who am only a vile
creature, remain before
Him crowned with pearls,
gold, and precious stones,
and by my crown mock his?*

—Elizabeth of Hungary,
1207-1231, Queen and
wife of Louis II

❀

HONOR: Proverbs 15:33   Matthew 11:28-30   John 2:11   John 5:22-23
John 17:1-4   Hebrews 2:7-9   Revelation 4:9-11

He will swallow up death forever.

The Sovereign Lord will wipe away the tears from all faces; he will remove the disgrace of his people from all the earth.

The Lord has spoken.

Isaiah 25:8

❋

VICTORIOUS: Psalm 44:1-8   Mark 16:4-6   John 16:33   Romans 8:31-39
1 Corinthians 15:51-58   Hebrews 2:14-15   Revelation 7:9-17

May

19_____

SUN	MON	TUES	WED	THURS	FRI	SAT

O God, let me not interrupt you with my chatter.
Let me listen, rather, to your still small voice.
                                            —Geddes MacGregor

Occasions for special prayer.

Ongoing prayer concerns.

_____

_____

_____

_____

_____

_____

_____

_____

_____

_____

_____

_____

_____

_____

By *The Holy Spirit*

BY CATHERINE MARSHALL

How often we have envied those who saw Jesus in the flesh, who talked to Him and touched Him! Sometimes in the midst of some personal crisis we have thought wistfully, "If only I could hear His voice right now!"

We wonder how anything could be more wonderful than the physical presence of our Lord. Yet Jesus never spoke lightly or thoughtlessly. And here we have His solemn word in His Last Supper talk with His apostles that there *is* something better—His presence in the form of the Holy Spirit....

What did He mean?

More, much more than the obvious fact that while Jesus was in the flesh He was subject to the fleshly limitations of time and space. Only those who managed to get within arm's reach could touch Him; only a few thousand at most could be within the sound of His voice.

But with the coming of the Helper, a new era would be dawning....

In the new era, Jesus is telling us, His glorified presence and His own resurrected life would be not only with us but also *in* us, progressively to transform us and our lives, working from the inside outwardly....

Here is a great mystery, difficult to put into words. It becomes real and practical to us only as we walk it out.

Catherine Marshall, *The Helper*, Chosen Books, 1978

Personal response/goal:

_____

_____

_____

_____

_____

_____

_____

_____

_____

_____

_____

THE HOLY SPIRIT

May

Spirit of God, descend
upon my heart.
    Wean it from earth;
through all its pulses move.
    Stoop to my weakness,
mighty as Thou art,
    And make me love Thee
as I ought to love.

    Hast Thou not bid us
love Thee, God and King?
    All, all Thine own: soul,
heart, and strength, and
mind!
    I see Thy cross—there
teach my heart to cling,
    O let me seek Thee, and
O let me find!

—George Croly, from
    the hymn *Spirit of God,
    Descend*

GOD: Genesis 1:2   Isaiah 28:5-6   Matthew 1:18-25   Matthew 3:16-17   Matthew 28:19
Acts 5:3-4   2 Corinthians 13:14

THE HOLY *May* SPIRIT

*Holy Spirit, think
through me till Your ideas
are my ideas.*

—Amy Carmichael,
1867-1951, missionary
to India and author)

❀

COUNSELOR: Numbers 11:10-30   John 14:16-18   John 14:24-27   John 15:26-27
Acts 20:22-24   Ephesians 1:17   Ephesians 3:4-5

THE HOLY *May* SPIRIT

God's Word tells us we
believers have two Intercessors
— Christ at the right hand of
God, and the Holy Spirit
dwelling in us. The Holy
Spirit takes our prayers when
we don't know what we
should pray for as we ought
and brings them to the Father
"according to the will of God"
(Romans 8:26-27). At times
when we cannot even put the
deep yearnings of our hearts
into words, we can rest
assured that the Holy Spirit is
interceding for us before the
throne of God according to
the Father's will.

—Evelyn Christenson, *What
   Happens When Women Pray*,
   Victor Books, 1991

❧

INTERCESSOR: Ezekiel 2:1-2   Romans 8:26-27   Romans 15:30   1 Corinthians 2:10-14
   1 Corinthians 14:13-17   2 Corinthians 3:12-18   Ephesians 6:18

THE HOLY *May* SPIRIT

O Holy Spirit of God,
who with Thy holy breath
doth cleanse the hearts and
minds of men, comforting
them when they be in sor-
row, leading them when
they be out of the way,
kindling them when they
be cold, knitting them
together when they be at
variance, and enriching
them with manifold gifts;
by whose working all
things live:

We beseech Thee to
maintain and daily to
increase the gifts which
Thou hast vouchsafed to
us; that with Thy light
before us and within us
we may pass through this
world without stumbling
and without straying; who
livest and reignest with
the Father and the Son,
everlastingly.

—Desiderius Erasmus,
   1469-1536, Dutch
   Renaissance reformist

❈

COMFORTER: Psalm 23:4   Psalm 143:10   Isaiah 57:15-19   Acts 9:31   Romans 9:1
                          2 Corinthians 1:3-7   Philippians 2:1-4

T H E   H O L Y   S P I R I T

May

Therefore every teacher of the law who has been instructed about the kingdom of heaven is like the owner of a house who brings out of his storeroom new treasures as well as old.

Matthew 13:52

❋

INSTRUCTOR: Genesis 41:37-40   Exodus 31:1-11   Deuteronomy 34:9
1 Chronicles 28:11-19   Job 32:7-8   Isaiah 30:1   Daniel 5:13-17

Your god may be your little Christian habit, the habit of prayer at stated times, or the habit of Bible reading. Watch how your Father will upset those times if you begin to worship your habit instead of what the habit symbolizes—I can't do that just now, I am praying; it is my hour with God. No, it is your hour with your habit.

—Oswald Chambers,
  My *Utmost for His Highest*,
  Discovery House
  Publishers, 1963

CONVICTOR: 2 Chronicles 24:20   Nehemiah 9:29-31   Isaiah 63:10   Zechariah 12:10
             Malachi 2:13-16   1 Thessalonians 1:4-6   Hebrews 6:4-6

Now if the ministry that brought death, which was engraved in letters on stone, came with glory, so that the Israelites could not look steadily at the face of Moses because of its glory, fading though it was, will not the ministry of the Spirit be even more glorious? If the ministry that condemns men is glorious, how much more glorious is the ministry that brings righteousness!

2 Corinthians 3:7-9

POWER: 1 Samuel 10:9-10   1 Samuel 16:13-14   2 Kings 2:7-14   Zechariah 4:6
Acts 1:8   Acts 4:31   2 Timothy 1:6-7

THE HOLY *May* SPIRIT

Today, if you hear His voice, do not harden your hearts as you did in the rebellion…

Hebrews 3:7b-8a

_____

_____

_____

_____

_____

_____

_____

_____

_____

_____

_____

_____

_____

_____

_____

_____

_____

_____

_____

_____

_____

_____

_____

_____

_____

_____

_____

_____

_____

❁

VOICE: Isaiah 48:16-18   Matthew 10:19-20   Luke 2:25-35   John 16:12-15
Acts 6:8-10   Acts 8:26-40   Revelation 22:17

THE HOLY SPIRIT

The one cornerstone of belief upon which the Society of Friends [Quakers] is built is the conviction that God does indeed communicate with each one of the spirits he has made, in a direct and living inbreathing of some measure of the breath of his own life; that he never leaves himself without a witness in the heart as well as in the surroundings of man; and that in order clearly to hear the divine voice thus speaking to us we need to be still; to be alone with him in the secret place of his presence; that all flesh should keep silence before him.

—Caroline Stephen, *Quaker Spirituality*, by
   Douglas V. Steere, Paulist Press, 1984)

GIFTS: Acts 2:1-4   Acts 2:38-39   Acts 11:11-18   Acts 13:52   Acts 19:1-7
Romans 15:5-6   1 Corinthians 12:4-13

These first Friends who trembled with a consciousness of God's nearness to them, and who rightly got the name of "Quakers," were in no doubt about the main fact. There was One nearer to them than breathing who "spoke to their condition." They felt the healing of God drop upon their souls. The whole creation had a new smell. They were "moved" to their tasks. They had dealings not with flesh and blood but with Spirit. They were called out from the plough and shop to enter upon a high commission. They at least had no doubt that "something in man" was in direct correspondence with God. They therefore eliminated mediators and seconds, and insisted upon the direct way and that which was first.

—Rufus M. Jones, *Quaker Spirituality*, by Douglas V. Steere, Paulist Press, 1984)

LIFE: Job 34:13-15   Psalm 104:29-31   John 6:63   Romans 8:1-2   Titus 3:3-8
James 2:26   1 Peter 3:18-22

THE HOLY *May* SPIRIT

O clear conscience!
How a little failing does
wound thee sore!

—Dante, *The Divine Comedy*

❧

LAW: Romans 8:1-17   1 Corinthians 6:12-20   Galatians 3:1-5   Galatians 5:16-18
Galatians 5:22-26   Galatians 6:7-10   Ephesians 4:30

THE HOLY *May* SPIRIT

And do not grieve the Holy Spirit of God, with whom you were sealed for the day of redemption. Get rid of all bitterness, rage and anger, brawling and slander, along with every form of malice. Be kind and compassionate to one another, forgiving each other, just as in Christ God forgave you.

Ephesians 4:30-32

JUNE

19_____

SUN	MON	TUES	WED	THURS	FRI	SAT

When you confess with Isaiah, "I am a man of unclean lips" (Isaiah 6:5), you will stand on the threshold of a victorious life. When you face the fact of your own inadequacy, your own failure, your own sinfulness, you have taken the first step toward gaining a glorious and wonderful personal victory that will carry you through the days of crisis that lie ahead.

—Billy Graham

Occasions for special prayer.

Ongoing prayer concerns.

_____   _____
_____   _____
_____   _____
_____   _____
_____   _____
_____   _____

Limitations

BY ANNIE CHAPMAN

One woman said to me, "I make all my decisions out of fear." Sometimes the fear of missing out controls her. Other times she fears getting left behind. Most often, however, she fears displeasing the people around her. When we live to please others, we're letting them set the limits on our lives.

Jesus pleased only one person, His Father. The Pharisees weren't pleased with Him. The crowds turned on Him. Even His closest disciples didn't always rave about His decisions. But He played His life to an audience of one, and could therefore disappoint others, yet have His heart at rest....

Have you confronted God about your limits, or are you trying to buy into the answers He's given others? God loves to be pursued. Hannah confronted God about her barrenness, and made such a fuss the priest assumed she was drunk. I admire a woman who will do battle with God like Hannah did. Her husband had taken his best shot at answering her pain: "Don't I mean more to you than ten sons?" But Hannah wanted to hear God's voice for herself. He responded, and she came away with a heart at peace....

My favorite example of someone whose limits didn't limit God is Helen Keller. Although blind and deaf, she graduated cum laude from Radcliffe, authored seven books and countless articles, traveled the continent educating people about the needs of the handicapped, toured in vaudeville, and made a silent movie.

A poem she wrote reveals how she saw her own limitations.

They took away what should have been my eyes.
(But I remembered Milton's *paradise*.)
They took away what should have been my ears.
(Beethoven came and wiped away my tears.)
They took away what should have been my tongue.
(But I had talked with God when I was young.)
He would not let them take away my soul.
(Possessing that I still possess the whole.)

Annie Chapman, *Smart Women Keep It Simple*, Bethany House Publishers, 1992

❦

Personal response/goal:

_____

_____

_____

_____

_____

_____

I wasn't God's first choice for what I've done for China.... I don't know who it was.... It must have been a man.... a well-educated man. I don't know what happened. Perhaps he died. Perhaps he wasn't willing.... And God looked down...and saw Gladys Aylward.... And God said, "Well, she's willing!"

If God has called you to China or any other place and you are sure in your own heart, let nothing deter you...remember it is God who has called you and it is the same as when he called Moses or Samuel.

—Gladys Aylward,
  1902-1970, missionary

ESTHER: Esther 2:1-23   Esther 3:1-11   Esther 4:1-17   Esther 5   Esther 7:1-10
Esther 8:1-13   Philippians 1:20-21

DEALING WITH *June* LIMITATIONS

"Here am I. Send me."

Isaiah 6:8

    *What is God asking me
to do? What is God asking
me to make a priority?
What things have I taken
on by my own choice and
not by God's leading?*

❧

MARY: Luke 1:26-56   Matthew 1:18-25   Luke 2:1-40   Matthew 2:1-15
Luke 2:41-52   John 19:25   Luke 1:38

We grow in the understanding of God while searching His Word with our heart; we grow in the faith in God during the trials of life.

❦

MIRIAM: Exodus 2:1-10 Exodus 14:13-31 Exodus 15:19-22 Numbers 12:1-15
Numbers 20:1 Micah 6:3-4

DEALING WITH *June* LIMITATIONS

*Create in me a pure
heart, O God,
   and renew a steadfast
spirit within me.*

Psalm 51:10

   *Each of the things we fail
at in life takes time and
effort on our part to correct.
From relationships that have
deteriorated, to poor eating
habits; from cluttered homes
and work spaces, to destruc-
tive, sinful habits. What a
blessing to know that God
works immediately. He can
remake our heart to be pure
and renew our weary spirit
in an instant, drawing us
back into communion with
Him. Why do we wait so
long to ask?*

❀

RAHAB: Joshua 2:1-21   Joshua 6:1-25   Matthew 1:5   Hebrews 11:30-31   James 2:25

DEALING WITH *June* LIMITATIONS

When the blind hymn writer Fanny J.
Crosby was told, "What a shame that you
are blind, dear." She replied, "Had I been
able to ask one thing of my Lord before I
was born, it would have been to be born
blind. You see, when I get to heaven, the
very first face I see will be that of my Jesus."

Later she wrote:
When my lifework is ended,
and I cross the swelling tide,
When the bright and glorious
morning I shall see,
I shall know my Redeemer
when I reach the other side,
And His smile will be
the first to welcome me.
I shall know Him.
I shall know Him.
And redeem'd by His side
I shall stand.
I shall know Him.
I shall know Him.
By the print of the nails in His hand.

—The story is a paraphrase of a well-known
account from the life of Fanny Crosby,
hymn is My *Savior First of All*

WEAKNESS: Romans 8:26   1 Corinthians 1:25   1 Corinthians 15:42-44
2 Corinthians 11:30   2 Corinthians 12:7-10   2 Corinthians 13:4   Hebrews 11:32-39

Better and sweeter than health, or friends, or money, or fame, or ease, or prosperity, is the adorable will of our God. It gilds the darkest hours with a divine halo, and sheds brightest sunshine on the gloomiest paths. He always reigns who has made it His kingdom, and nothing can go amiss to Him. Surely, then, it is only a glorious privilege that is opening before you, when I tell you that the first step you must take in order to enter into the life hid with Christ in God, is that of entire consecration... and I can assure you from the universal testimony of all who have tried it, that you will find it the happiest place you have ever entered yet.

—Hannah Whitall Smith, *The Christian's Secret of a Happy Life*, Barbour and Company, Inc., 1990

SARAH: Genesis 11:29–12:5   Genesis 12:10-20   Genesis 17:15-22   Genesis 18:1-15
Genesis 20:1-17   Genesis 21:1-6   1 Peter 3:1-6

Who am I? This or the other?
Am I one person today and tomorrow another?
Am I both at once? A hypocrite before others
And before myself a contemptible woebegone weakling?
Or is something within me still like a beaten army,
Fleeing in disorder from victory already achieved?
Who am I? they mock me, these lonely questions of mine,
Whoever I am, Thou knowest,
O God, I am Thine!

—Dietrich Bonhoeffer, 1906-1945, German preacher who
   was imprisoned and later killed by the Nazis.

HANNAH: 1 Samuel 1:1–2:11   1 Samuel 2:18-21   1 Samuel 2:26   1 Samuel 3:1-21
1 Samuel 7:15-17   Galatians 4:27

DEALING WITH *June* LIMITATIONS

He that is down needs fear no fall
He that is low, no pride:
He that is humble ever shall
Have God to be his guide.

I am content with what I have,
Little be it or much:
And, Lord, contentment still I crave,
Because Thou savest such.

—John Bunyan, 1628-1688,
   English clergyman and author

RUTH: Ruth 1:1-18   Ruth 2:1-13   Ruth 2:19-23   Ruth 3:1-13   Ruth 4:1-17
Psalm 18:25   Matthew 1:5

DEALING WITH *June* LIMITATIONS

*If God could be
reached only through
intellect, then where
would the brain-damaged,
the mentally retarded, the
little child be? When
Jesus put the little child in
the midst of His disciples,
He did not tell the little
child to become like His
disciples; He told the
disciples to become like
the little child.*

—Ruth Bell Graham,
  It's My Turn, Fleming H.
  Revell, 1982

❧

CHILDLIKE: Matthew 18:1-6   Matthew 19:13-15   Matthew 21:14-16   Luke 10:21
Romans 8:16-17   Romans 16:19   Ephesians 5:1-2

There was a poor widow woman in the countryside, as I came through, that was worth many of you. She was asked how she did in this evil time. "I do very well," she said. "I get more of one verse of the Bible now than I did of all the Bible in times past. He hath cast me the keys to the pantry door, and bidden me take my fill."

—Alexander Peden

WIDOWS: Deuteronomy 24:19-22   1 Kings 17:1-24   Mark 12:41-44
Luke 2:36-38   Luke 7:11-15   Psalm 146:5-9

Roadside sign in Kentucky: "Pray for a good harvest, but keep on hoeing."

✿

DEBORAH: Deuteronomy 16:18-20 Judges 2:18-19 Judges 4:4-10 Judges 4:12-24
Judges 5:1-13 Judges 6:1 Proverbs 31:8-9

*And after you
have done every-
thing, to stand.*

Ephesians 6:13

❀

MANY MARYS: Luke 8:1-3   Matthew 27:58-61   John 20:1-18   Luke 10:38-42
John 12:1-8   John 11:1-45   Romans 12:9-13

July

19_____

SUN	MON	TUES	WED	THURS	FRI	SAT

"Come to me, all you who are weary and burdened, and I will give you rest. Take my yoke upon you and learn from me, for I am gentle and humble in heart, and you will find rest for your souls. For my yoke is easy and my burden is light."

—*Matthew 11:28-30*

Occasions for special prayer.

Ongoing prayer concerns.

BY DALE EVANS ROGERS

Suffering

It was a woman to whom Jesus Christ appeared in His resurrection body: Mary Magdalene, the tormented woman whom Jesus cured of what must have been demonic possession. She must have suffered with mental illness for years, before Jesus healed her and restored her sanity. Mary Magdalene became one of the most devoted women disciples, following Jesus to the very foot of the Cross.

Mary Magdalene was present at the trial in Pilate's hall, when the so-called religious leaders of the time shouted for the crucifixion of her Master. She watched with a broken heart the agonies of Christ on the Cross. As the song says, she was there when they crucified her Lord. She was last at the Cross and first at the garden tomb. She witnessed the most important event in world history, and the event upon which Christianity is based: the Resurrection of Jesus Christ. The disciples came and saw that the stone had been rolled away, peeked in, and then do you know what they did? They went home! But not Mary Magdalene. She stood outside the tomb and cried, and as she wept, two angels appeared to her and asked her most tenderly, "Woman, why are you weeping?" Oh, the heartbreak, the pathos in this woman when she replied, "Because they have taken away my Lord, and I do not know where they have laid Him" (John 20:13, RSV).

God has given women the depth of compassion to weep for those we love. But He rewards us beyond our understanding, when He calls us by name, as He did this woman. "Woman, why are you weeping?" Then when she heard the voice she knew so well say her name Mary, she answered Him instantly with "Rabboni!" which means "Teacher," the strongest expression of love and respect.

Oh, what Christ can do for a woman! He is able to take our tormented souls and give us peace. Mary Magdalene reminds me that once He heals us, there are so many ways we can serve Him, but the most important of all is witnessing to others of His resurrection power.

Dale Evans Rogers, *Woman*, Fleming H. Revell, 1980

※

Personal response/goal:

_____

_____

_____

_____

_____

_____

S U F F E R I N G

Therefore, since Christ suffered in his body, arm yourselves also with the same attitude, because he who has suffered in his body is done with sin. As a result, he does not live the rest of his earthly life for evil human desires, but rather for the will of God.

1 Peter 4:1-2

❧

SUFFERING: Job 30:15-20   Psalm 22:23-24   Psalm 119:49-50   Isaiah 38:15-20
Isaiah 53:3, 11   Matthew 9:36   Romans 5:3-5

We thank Thee, Lord, for the glory of the late days and the excellent face of Thy sun. We thank Thee for good news received. We thank Thee for the pleasures we have enjoyed and for those we have been able to confer. And now, when the clouds gather and rain impends over the forest and our house, permit us not to be cast down; let us not lose the savour of past mercies and past pleasures; but, like the voice of a bird singing in the rain, let grateful memory survive in the hour of darkness.

—Robert Louis Stevenson,
 1850-1894, Scottish author

❉

TROUBLE: Job 2:10   Job 4:1-5   Psalm 10:14   Psalm 32:6-7   Psalm 138:7-8
Matthew 13:18-23   John 16:33

We give back to You,
O God, those whom You
gave to us. You did not lose
them when You gave them to
us and we do not lose them
by their return to You.

Your dear Son has taught
us that life is eternal and love
cannot die, so death is only
an horizon and an horizon is
only the limit of our sight.
Open our eyes to see more
clearly and draw us close to
You that we may know that
we are nearer to our loved
ones who are with You. You
have told us that You are
preparing a place for us;
prepare us also for that happy
place, that where You are we
may also be always, O dear
Lord of life and death.

—William Penn, 1644-1718,
   English Quaker and
   American colonist

DEATH: Psalm 23:4   Psalm 89:48   Psalm 116:15   Proverbs 14:32   Isaiah 57:1-2
Ezekiel 18:23, 32   Romans 8:38-39

Grieving is work. Hard work. And so often, our first almost unconscious act of participation must be to accept ourselves in that beginning traumatic stage and feel no guilt for seeming to be so helpless, so faithless, so self-concerned. The pain is still too sharp. Our bodies as well as our minds may be in shock. We are not to blame for this. We are human. To expect anyone who has loved to walk away from an open grave in good, strong spirits—no matter how deeply rooted faith is—is as ridiculous as to expect a patient to get up off an operating table after major surgery and walk away.

—Eugenia Price, *Getting Through the Night*, Doubleday, 1982

GRIEF: Psalm 88:8-9   Ecclesiastes 3:1-8   Lamentations 3:25-26, 32-33   Matthew 5:4
John 16:20-22   Romans 12:15   Revelation 21:1-5

No human being—no other human being on earth—can understand the weight of your burden. But here is the key: God does understand the exact extent and pain of your grief because He created you in the first place— as you are. He didn't create you as someone else is; He created you as you are. Say aloud to Him this minute: "Thou knowest my downsitting and mine uprising, thou understandest my thoughts afar off. Thou compassest my path and my lying down, and art acquainted with all my ways."

And remember that this Creator God says of himself where you are concerned: "I am understanding."

He isn't prodding you into feeling better by reminding you that He has the ability to understand human grief, He is stating another more awesome fact. He is succinctly characterizing himself to you: "I am understanding."

—Eugenia Price, *Getting Through the Night*, Doubleday, 1982

✻

I AM: John 6:35   John 8:12   John 10:7-10   John 10:11-14   John 11:25
John 14:6   John 15:5

S U F F E R I N G

July

*Just as I know that because
of who I am — I will fail,
I also know that because
of who You are — I will
inevitably succeed.*

_____

_____

_____

_____

_____

_____

_____

_____

_____

_____

_____

_____

_____

_____

_____

_____

_____

_____

_____

_____

_____

_____

_____

_____

_____

_____

_____

_____

_____

_____

❧

DOUBT: Numbers 20:5   Joshua 7:7   1 Samuel 4:3   Job 3:11-13   Jeremiah 20:18
Matthew 14:31   Romans 9:20-21

S U F F E R I N G
July

"My ears had heard of you
but now my eyes have seen you.
Therefore I despise myself
and repent in dust and ashes."

  The Lord blessed the latter part
of Job's life more than the first.

Job 42:5-6, 12

❧

REVERENCE: Psalm 5:7   Daniel 6:26-27   Acts 10:25-26   2 Corinthians 7:1
Ephesians 5:21   Hebrews 12:28-29   Revelation 11:18

SU *July* RING

*My spirit has become
dry because it forgets to
feed on You.*

—John of the Cross,
    1542-1591, Spanish poet

SUSTENANCE: Psalm 41:2-4   Psalm 55:22   Psalm 119:174-176   Psalm 121
Isaiah 46:4   1 Corinthians 1:8-9   Jude 24-25

O Lord, let me not henceforth desire health or life except to spend them for You and with You. You alone know what is good for me; do therefore what seems best to You. Give to me or take from me; I desire to adore equally all that comes to me from You, my Lord and God.

—Blaise Pascal, 1623-1662, French mathematician and theologian who suffered excruciating headache pain

PAUL: Acts 7:59–8:3   Acts 9:1-22   Acts 14:19-20   Acts 16:19-31   Acts 21:12-14
Acts 23:10-11   Romans 8:18

SUFFERING *July*

In my attempts to promote the comfort of my family, the quiet of my spirit has been disturbed...This is of great importance, to watch carefully, — now I am so weak — not to over fatigue myself, because then I cannot contribute to the pleasure of others; and a placid face and a gentle tone will make my family more happy than anything else I can do for them.

—Elizabeth T. King, 1820-1856

GROWTH: Job 8:8-9   Psalm 89:15   Psalm 119:71-73   Matthew 11:25-26   Mark 9:24
2 Timothy 3:1-7   1 John 5:3-5

SU F F E R I N G

Healing begins with trust.
If you do not trust God, then
you cannot take Him at His
Word. And if you cannot take
Him at His Word, then you are
refusing the only certain means
of healing.

—Kay Arthur, *Lord, Heal My*
  Hurts, Harvest House, 1989

HEALING: Job 5:18   Isaiah 30:26   Jeremiah 17:14   Hosea 6:1
Mark 5:34   Acts 3:16

S U F F E R I N G

July

It matters not
if the world has heard
or approves or understands....
The only applause
we're meant to seek
is that of nail-scarred hands.

—B.J. Hoff, *Faces in the Crowd,*
   Warner Press, 1993

***

APPROVAL: Psalm 62:1-2   John 5:44   John 6:26-27   Romans 12:2
1 Corinthians 3:7-8   2 Corinthians 10:18   Galatians 1:10

19_____

SUN	MON	TUES	WED	THURS	FRI	SAT

We belittle God when we beg for crumbs, while He stands before us in the Person of Jesus Christ and declares himself to be the entire bread of life! Far from expecting too much, we expect too little.

—Eugenia Price

Occasions for special prayer.

_____

_____

_____

_____

_____

_____

_____

Ongoing prayer concerns.

_____

_____

_____

_____

_____

_____

_____

By HANNAH WHITALL SMITH

What Is Faith

Your idea of faith, I suppose, has been something like this. You have looked upon it as in some way a sort of thing—either a religious exercise of soul, or an inward, gracious disposition of heart; something tangible, in fact, which, when you have secured it, you can look at and rejoice over, and use as a passport to God's favor, or a coin with which to purchase His gifts. And you have been praying for faith, expecting all the while to get something like this; and never having received any such thing, you are insisting upon it that you have no faith. Now faith, in fact, is not in the least like this. It is nothing at all tangible. It is simply believing God; and, like sight, it is nothing apart from its object. You might as well shut your eyes and look inside to see whether you have sight, as to look inside to discover whether you have faith. You see something, and thus know that you have sight; you believe something, and thus know that you have faith. For as sight is only seeing, so faith is only believing. And as the only thing necessary about sight is that you see the thing as it is, so the only necessary thing about faith is that you believe the thing as it is. The virtue does not lie in your believing, but in the thing you believe.

Hannah Whitall Smith, *Eerdman's Book of Christian Classics,* "What Faith Really Is," William B. Eerdmans Publishing Company, 1985

Personal response/goal:

_____

_____

_____

_____

_____

_____

_____

_____

_____

_____

_____

_____

_____

_____

AUGUST

FAITH

*For if God...did not
spare the ancient world
when he brought the flood
on its ungodly people, but
protected Noah, a preacher
of righteousness, and seven
others; if he condemned the
cities of Sodom and
Gomorrah by burning them
to ashes, and made them
an example of what is going
to happen to the ungodly;
and if he rescued Lot, a
righteous man, who was
distressed by the filthy lives
of lawless men...if this is so,
then the Lord knows how to
rescue godly men from trials
and to hold the unrighteous
for the day of judgment,
while continuing their
punishment.*

2 Peter 2:4-9,
selected portions

SALVATION: Exodus 15:2   Psalm 40:6-10   Psalm 69:13   Psalm 98:1-3   Isaiah 33:6
Isaiah 51:6   Acts 4:12

August
FAITH

One sure way of not asking amiss is to know God's Word, the Bible. If God calls it sin, don't insult Him by asking about it.

—Evelyn Christenson,
  What Happens When Women Pray,
  Victor Books, 1991

WILL: Mark 3:34-35   Romans 8:26-27   Romans 12:2   1 Thessalonians 4:3-8
1 Thessalonians 5:16-18   1 Peter 2:13-17   1 Peter 4:19

It is possible that some who read these words may have a complaint against God. A controversy of long standing has come between your soul and His grace. If you were to say the word that is trembling on your lips, you would say to him, "Why have you dealt with me this way?" Then dare to say, with reverence and with boldness, all that is in your heart.

—David M'Intyre,
   The Hidden Life of Prayer,
   Bethany House Publishers, 1993

❋

STRUGGLES: Genesis 32:23-30   Psalm 13:1-2   Romans 15:30   Ephesians 6:10-12
Colossians 1:28-29   Colossians 4:12   Hebrews 12:4

August

FAITH

Has God put before you an open door? Are you hesitating, perhaps rebelling or holding back because of fear, when God is challenging, "Look, here's an open door, wouldn't you like to walk through it for Me? This is My will for you."

Oh, answer Him, "Lord, here I am. There is no friction between my will and Yours. Whatever You have for me, I know that You will give me enough strength, enough grace. I know You will give me all that I need. Lord, I am ready to do Your will."

—Evelyn Christenson, *What Happens When Women Pray*, Victor Books, 1991

SUBMISSION: 2 Corinthians 8:11-12   Colossians 2:20-22   Colossians 3:18
Hebrews 5:7   Hebrews 12:9   James 3:17   James 4:7-8

August

Understanding is the reward of faith. Therefore seek not to understand that you may believe, but believe that you may understand.

—Augustine, 354-430,
  early philosopher and
  religious leader

✿

FAITH: Matthew 8:5-13   Matthew 8:23-27   Matthew 15:21-28   Matthew 16:5-12
Matthew 17:20   Matthew 21:21-22   Matthew 24:10-13

F A I T H
August

My words fly up, my
thoughts stay below;
  Words without thoughts
never to heaven go.

—William Shakespeare,
  1564-1616, English
  dramatist and poet

THOUGHTS: Psalm 10:4   Psalm 92:5   Psalm 139:1-6   Psalm 139:23-24   Amos 4:13
Hebrews 3:1-3   Hebrews 4:12-13

FAITH August

Worrying is carrying tomorrow's load with today's strength—carrying two days at once. It is moving into tomorrow ahead of time. Worrying does not empty tomorrow of its sorrow—it empties today of its strength.

—Corrie ten Boom, *He Cares, He Comforts,* Fleming H. Revell, 1977

WORRY: Psalm 112:1-8   Matthew 6:25-34   Matthew 13:22   Luke 10:41-42
Luke 21:12-15   1 Corinthians 7:32-38   Jude 22

To be sure, God often more than answers prayer. He grants them not only what they ask, but often connects other blessings with it.

—Charles G. Finney, 1792-1875, *Principles of Prayer*

❦

DOUBT: Deuteronomy 4:31   Nehemiah 9:31   1 Corinthians 1:18-25
1 Corinthians 1:26-31   2 Corinthians 4:8-9   Matthew 11:27   John 20:24-25

Faith F A I T H *August*

*Now faith is being
sure of what we hope
for and certain of
what we do not see.*

Hebrews 11:1

_____

_____

_____

_____

_____

_____

_____

_____

_____

_____

_____

_____

_____

_____

_____

_____

_____

_____

_____

_____

_____

_____

_____

_____

_____

*

CERTAINTY: Psalm 19:9   Psalm 69:13   Habakkuk 2:3   Matthew 10:42   John 17:8
2 Corinthians 13:4   Hebrews 6:11-12

August

FAITH

The world has yet to see what
God can do with a man
completely dedicated to Him.

—Dwight L. Moody, 1837-1899,
   American evangelist

_____

_____

_____

_____

_____

_____

_____

_____

_____

_____

_____

_____

_____

_____

_____

_____

_____

_____

_____

_____

_____

_____

_____

_____

✿

QUESTIONS: 1 Kings 10:1-9   Matthew 21:23-27   Matthew 22:34-46   Mark 12:18-27
               Luke 20:20-26   John 8:1-11   Luke 23:8-9

I was discussing [God's will] with a faculty wife one day, and she said, "Look, girl, I'd feel like a pawn in God's hand if I ever prayed that way."

I thought for a minute. Wow! Maybe so. Then I said, "You know, maybe the greatest privilege in the whole world would be for me to be a pawn in the hands of God, a pawn who never makes a mistake. Just think, I'd never have to 'trial and error' anything. I'd never fall on my face (which I do very frequently). If God were in control of my every action, I would never do anything wrong. What a privilege to be a pawn in God's hands!"

—Evelyn Christenson, *What Happens When Women Pray,* Victor Books, 1991

RESTING: Exodus 33:14   Deuteronomy 33:12   Joshua 21:44-45   Nehemiah 9:28
Psalm 62:1-2   Jeremiah 6:16   1 John 3:19-20

FAITH

*Trust in the Lord with
all your heart
    and lean not on your
own understanding;
    in all your ways
acknowledge him,
    and he will make your
paths straight.*

Proverbs 3:5

TRUST: Psalm 9:10   Psalm 20:7-8   Psalm 25   Psalm 37:3-5   Psalm 56:3-4
Psalm 62:7-8   Psalm 125:1-2

September

19____

SUN	MON	TUES	WED	THURS	FRI	SAT

Prayer is like incense. It costs a great deal. It doesn't seem to accomplish much (as we mortals assess things). It soon dissipates. But God likes the smell. It was God's idea to arrange the work of the tabernacle to include a special altar for incense. We can be pretty sure He included all that was necessary and nothing that was unnecessary.

—Elisabeth Elliot

Occasions for special prayer.

Ongoing prayer concerns.

"Mommy, Mommy, Mommy, Mommy, Mommy, Mommy." Marty's persistence matched his rhythmic tugging on my blouse's hem.

I felt like screaming. In fact, I did.

To a little guy my response was probably similar to the release of Mt. St. Helens as I erupted, "What?!"

Why a mother waits so long to respond and allows the repetition to light her lava is beyond me. I only know that after spewing all over him I felt terrible...and so did he.

Where did all this volcanic anger come from? I seemed to always be upset at something or someone. Often my reactions were greater than the situation called for. I realized that Marty's little-child ways didn't deserve such strong responses....

During a prayer time, as I cried out to the Lord for help with my temper, especially with my son, an idea formed I believe was heaven-sent because it made a difference.

I was to pray with Marty before I administered any form of discipline. Sometimes those prayers sounded strange and strained as I almost shouted, "Dear Lord, help this miserable little boy and help his miserable mommy who wants so desperately to raise him in a way that would honor You."

By the time I said "amen," I was almost a reasonable person. I was able to see past my emotions and do what was in Marty's best interest.

Sometimes he needed a firm hand, but he was dealt with in love instead of anger, and the moment drew us together instead of tearing us apart. Many times all he needed was time and a mother's tender touch.

But one day that boy really ticked me off! I remember heading across the room for him like a high-speed locomotive, steam coming out all sides. I had one goal and intent—get the kid, get the kid, get the kid!

Just as I loomed over him, his eyes the size of saucers, he held up one hand and yelled, "Let's pray!"

Marty had learned a valuable lesson in life: "When Mommy talks to Jesus, we're all a lot better off."

Who lights your lava?

Patsy Clairmont, *God Uses Cracked Pots*, Focus on the Family, 1991

Personal response/goal:

_____

_____

_____

_____

_____

_____

September

ANGER

It is sometimes thought that the emotions are the governing power in our nature. But I think all of us know, as a matter of practical experience, that there is something within us, behind our emotions and behind our wishes, an independent self, that, after all, decides everything and controls everything. Our emotions belong to us, and are suffered and enjoyed by us, but they are not ourselves; and if God is to take possession of us, it must be into this central will or personality that He enters. If, then, He is reigning there by the power of His Spirit, all the rest of our nature must come under His sway; and as the will is, so is the man.

—Hannah Whitall Smith,
*The Christian's Secret of a
Happy Life*, Barbour and
Company, Inc., 1990

EMOTIONS: 1 Samuel 16:14-23   1 Samuel 20:30-42   1 Kings 19:1-18   Psalm 137
Jonah 3:10–4:11   Acts 7:54-58   Ephesians 4:26-27

September

ANGER

Justifiable or not, anger is never to control us. We are to be controlled by the Spirit of God; therefore, our response must be according to His total character. The moment we are manifesting anything but His heart, we are in trouble.

—Kay Arthur, *Lord, Heal My Hurts*, Harvest House Publishers, 1989

CONTROL: Proverbs 16:32 Proverbs 29:11 Galatians 5:22-25 Philippians 3:17-21
Titus 2:3-5 1 Peter 4:7-8 2 Peter 1:5-8

September

Whenever you are angry, be assured that it is not only a present evil, but that you have increased a habit.

—Epictetus, Greek philosopher

TEMPERAMENT: Psalm 37:7-8   Proverbs 29:22   Ecclesiastes 7:9   2 Corinthians 12:20
Galatians 5:19-21   Ephesians 4:29-32   Colossians 3:5-10

September

Love your enemies and pray for those who perse-cute you, that you may be sons of your Father in heaven. He causes his sun to rise on the evil and the good, and sends rain on the righteous and the unrighteous. If you love those who love you, what reward will you get? Are not even the tax collectors doing that? And if you greet only your brothers, what are you doing more than others? Do not even pagans do that? Be per-fect, therefore, as your heavenly Father is perfect.

Matthew 5:44-48

❋

ENEMIES: Exodus 23:4-5   Deuteronomy 23:14   Joshua 7:10-13   Proverbs 16:7
Proverbs 24:17   Proverbs 25:21   Romans 12:17-21

September
ANGER

A Christian will find it cheaper
to pardon than to resent.
Forgiveness saves the expense of
anger, the cost of hatred, the
waste of spirits.

—Hannah More, 1745-1833, writer

✿

GRUDGES: Genesis 27:41   Genesis 50:15   Leviticus 19:18   Judges 15:6-8
Judges 16:28-30   Mark 6:19-20   Romans 12:19

September

Epitaph seen on a stone in a country cemetery: "Here lies my darling husband, Walter. May he rest in peace...until we meet again."

❃

HUSBANDS: Proverbs 15:17   Proverbs 19:13-14   Proverbs 21:9   Proverbs 21:19
Proverbs 25:23-24   Proverbs 30:33   Proverbs 31:10

September

*If you had known
what these words mean,
"I desire mercy, not
sacrifice," you would
not have condemned
the innocent.*

Matthew 12:7

❀

MERCY: 2 Samuel 24:14   Psalm 123:2   Micah 6:8   Matthew 5:7   Romans 12:6-13
Colossians 3:12-14   Jude 22-23

ANGER

My dear brothers, take note of this: Everyone should be quick to listen, slow to speak and slow to become angry, for man's anger does not bring about the righteous life that God desires.

James 1:19-20

❧

PATIENCE: Proverbs 14:29   Proverbs 15:18   Proverbs 19:11   Proverbs 25:15
Matthew 18:23-35   Romans 12:1-4   1 Thessalonians 5:14-18

September

Sometimes forgiveness comes easily. At other times the hurt is so deep and the anger so deserved that we must wrestle hard and long in prayer before we can finally come to honest terms with God and ourselves. Don't give up. Will to forgive. Keep praying for deliverance from the pain. Keep seeking God's healing. Eventually the devil must give ground.

—Janette Oke

COST: 1 Chronicles 21:24   Luke 14:28-33   Luke 19:8-10   1 Corinthians 3:10-15
1 Corinthians 6:19-20   1 Corinthians 7:23   Revelation 21:6

September

ANGER

We don't pray, "Forgive us our trespasses as we forgive those who ask us to." We say, "as we forgive those who trespass against us." It's not a matter of ignoring what's been done. When God forgives He doesn't merely overlook our trespasses. He doesn't ask us to overlook others' trespasses either—He asks us to forgive them. So that means our Christian obligation is to forgive anybody who has invaded our rights, our territory, our comfort, our self-image, whether they acknowledge the invasion or not.

—Elisabeth Elliot, *Love Has a Price Tag*, Christian Herald Books, 1979

OBLIGATION: Matthew 6:12-15   Matthew 18:21-22   Mark 11:25   Luke 6:37-42
Luke 11:4   Luke 17:1-5   Luke 23:34

September

I believe that if we could only see beforehand what it is that our heavenly Father means us to be, — the soul beauty and perfection and glory, the glorious and lovely spiritual body that this soul is to dwell in through all eternity — if we could have a glimpse of this, we should not grudge all the trouble and pains He is taking with us now, to bring us up to that ideal, which is His thought of us.

—Annie Keary, 1825-1879

AT GOD: Job 1:8–3:16   Job 6:1-10   Job 10:1-18   Job 40:1-14   Job 42:1-6

September

Do we dare pray, "Lord, reveal to me my hypocrisies"? He surely will, if we ask.

❀

HYPOCRISY: Psalm 26:4   Matthew 6:2-8   Matthew 6:16-18   Matthew 7:3-5
Matthew 23:25-28   Luke 12:1-3   1 Peter 2:1-3

October

19_____

SUN	MON	TUES	WED	THURS	FRI	SAT

"We do not pray answers, we pray requests."

Do you see the difference? When we pray answers, we're demanding that God do something and we're telling Him we want it done now— "just the way we want it, Lord." When we're bringing our requests to Him, we're saying, "Lord, here's the need"—the circumstance, the person, whatever it may be; then we ask Him to answer according to His omniscient will.

—Evelyn Christenson

Occasions for special prayer.

_____

_____

_____

_____

_____

_____

Ongoing prayer concerns.

_____

_____

_____

_____

_____

_____

Intercession

BY JANETTE OKE

My husband, Edward, is the Academic Dean at Rocky Mountain College, a school for biblical studies. I was reminded once again upon hearing the moving testimony of one of the students of the importance of prayer—and of grandmothers. The young man sharing with us had traveled a rough and rebellious road but at one point in the telling of his story, he stopped, smiled and said, "But I had a grandmother who just wouldn't stop praying for me." Through a series of God-directed events in his life, the young man discovered for himself that God is real and that He cares. Mike is now training to be a minister.

It is a wonderful privilege to be a grandmother. It is especially meaningful to know that as a grandmother, you can be another strong line of defense in the spiritual battle in the life of each of your grandchildren.

Sometimes we look at our world or listen to the news reports and feel that our prize possessions have been tossed on the roiling seas of Satan's fury. But our God is still the same God who snatched Moses from the bulrushes and made the ranting Pharaoh his protector rather than his murderer. He is still the same God who made the hungry lions Daniel's companions in the dark den rather than his devourers. The list goes on and on. God has not changed. We can still trust those we love to His care.

As grandparents we have the wonderful privilege—and responsibility—to remember each grandchild daily. We can surround them with the protection of prayer when they are still too young to be saying prayers of their own. As they continue to grow, we can ask for God's help when they are meeting temptation, and we can build prayer walls that hold Satan at bay. We can ask for wisdom and good judgment in their decision making and choosing of friends. We can begin our day with prayer for their safekeeping, physically, but especially spiritually. We can end the day with a prayer for their protection through the night hours. And in those difficult, trying, testing times that they may face, we can add additional short prayers as we go about our duties of the day or have interruptions to our sleep in the night hours.

One can never pray too much for those he loves. They can never have too many prayers whispered on their behalf. Uphold them, defend them, put up prayer walls, and build bridges, all in Jesus' name. And let them know that you are praying for them. It's part of a Christian's expression of love.

❦

Personal response/goal:

_____

_____

_____

_____

_____

October

A child's kiss
Set on thy sighing lips, shall make thee glad;
A poor man served by thee, shall make thee rich;
A sick man helped by thee, shall make thee strong;
Thou shalt be served thyself by every sense
Of service which thou renderest.

—Elizabeth Barrett Browning, 1806-1861, English poet

FOR OTHERS: Job 42:7-9   Romans 10:1-3   1 Corinthians 10:32-33
2 Thessalonians 1:11-12   1 Timothy 2:1-4   2 Timothy 3:14-17   James 5:16

Lord, guard me from the type of mother-love that would plead for Your total protection, total ease, and total fulfillment for my children. I realize that much must be learned through trials, testings, and thwarted desires. May I not demand a wrapped-in-cotton existence that would lead to a shallow life and entrance to heaven of only a spiritual shell of a man.

—Janette Oke

FOR PROTECTION: Psalm 12:5-8   Psalm 20:1-2   Psalm 91:14-16   Proverbs 4:6
Jeremiah 49:11   John 17:11-12, 15   2 Thessalonians 3:3

But do not forget this one thing, dear friends: With the Lord a day is like a thousand years, and a thousand years are like a day. The Lord is not slow in keeping his promise, as some understand slowness. He is patient with you, not wanting anyone to perish, but everyone to come to repentance.

2 Peter 3:8-9

HEAVEN: Isaiah 65:17-19   Luke 12:32-34   John 14:1-3   Philippians 1:21-24
1 Peter 1:3-9   2 Peter 3:11-13   Revelation 22:20

The prayer movement that is occurring in this country is unlike anything I've seen in my lifetime. Millions of believers have been asking the Lord to heal our land, to preserve our families, and to cleanse us from sin and wickedness. They have met in their homes, in places of business, in churches, on the Capitol steps, at city halls around the nation, and on thousands of school campuses. Heaven must be echoing with the sweet sound of these petitions coming from so many sincere Christians who are concerned about the moral crisis fomenting around us.

—Dr. James C. Dobson,
 Focus on the Family
 Newsletter, January 1995

FOR REVIVAL: 1 Kings 8:46-51   Psalm 80:14-19   Psalm 85   Jeremiah 5:3-5
Luke 16:19-31   Acts 3:19-21   Acts 17:30-31

Pray also for me, that whenever I open my mouth, words may be given me so that I will fearlessly make known the mystery of the gospel, for which I am an ambassador in chains. Pray that I may declare it fearlessly, as I should.

Ephesians 6:19-20

Lord, we pray these words of Paul's for each of those whom You have called into service for You. Bless our pastor, our missionaries, those who teach about You in our colleges, those Christians in government buildings, those with burdens to reach the children in our neighborhoods, those who sing for You, those who write for You, those who speak on Your behalf in any setting; bless each one with this prayer.

And guard them from submitting to temptation.

FOR LEADERS: John 17   Romans 15:17-18   1 Corinthians 2:6-10   Colossians 4:3-4
1 Thessalonians 5:25   2 Thessalonians 3:1-2   Hebrews 13:18-19

October

INTERCESSION

*As for me, far be it
from me that I should sin
against the Lord by failing
to pray for you. And I
will teach you the way
that is good and right.*

1 Samuel 12:23

_____

_____

_____

_____

_____

_____

_____

_____

_____

_____

_____

_____

_____

_____

_____

_____

_____

_____

_____

_____

_____

_____

❈

CHILDREN: Proverbs 19:18   Proverbs 20:11   Proverbs 22:6   Proverbs 22:15
Proverbs 23:13   Proverbs 29:17

The Gulf Stream is in the ocean, and yet it is not a part of it. Believers are in the world, and yet they must not be absorbed by it. The Gulf Stream maintains its warm temperatures even in the icy water of the North Atlantic. If Christians are to fulfill their purposes in the world they must not be chilled by the indifferent, godless society in which they live.

—Billy Graham,
  The Hour of Decision, 1953

❧

FOR SOCIETY: Exodus 32:11-14   1 Kings 8:30   Psalm 100:3   Psalm 122:6-9
Hebrews 6:9-12   Jude 3-10   Revelation 21:3

October

INTERCESSION

O God, help us not to despise or oppose what we do not understand.

—William Penn, 1644-
    1718, English Quaker
    and American colonist

🌸

FOR UNDERSTANDING: Mark 12:32-33   Ephesians 1:7-10   Ephesians 4:17-24
    Philippians 4:7   Colossians 1:9-12   Colossians 2:2-7   Philemon 6

Too many people do not care what happens as long as it does not happen to them.

—William Howard Taft,
1857-1930,
27th US President

❀

FOR THE SICK AND SUFFERING: Matthew 4:35-41   Luke 10:30-37   Luke 18:1-8
John 10:11-13   John 21:15-17   1 Timothy 3:5   1 Peter 5:2-4

The best thing a woman can do for her husband is to make it easy for him to do the will of God.

—Elisabeth Elliot, author and wife of martyred missionary

CAUTIONS: Leviticus 25:17   Proverbs 10:17   Proverbs 11:25   Ecclesiastes 7:21-22
Matthew 5:19   Matthew 5:39-42   Matthew 7:12

An occult high priest was quoted in our local newspaper as saying that the churches of America have given up the supernatural. They don't deal in the supernatural; they just deal in plans and programs and social action. He said that every human being is created with a supernatural vacuum, and since Christians aren't doing anything in the realm of the supernatural, he feels that witchcraft is a reasonable substitute for Christianity.

—Evelyn Christenson, *What Happens When Women Pray*, Victor Books, 1991

SPIRITUAL WAR: Matthew 4:1-11   Matthew 13:37-43   Matthew 18:10
Acts 10:37-38   Ephesians 6:12   2 Timothy 2:22-26   1 Peter 5:8-9

Teach me to kneel in spirit before all whom it is my privilege to serve, because they are Your children: to look for the family likeness, however homely or unspiritual the appearance of those to whom I am sent; however lowly my sphere of service and their needs may be…

Come, Lord! come with me: see with my eyes: hear with my ears: think with my mind: love with my heart— in all the situations of my life. Work with my hands: my strength. Take, cleanse, possess, inhabit, my will, my understanding, my love.

Take me where You will, to do what You will, in Your way.

For where You are, there would Your servant be.

—Evelyn Underhill,
  1875-1941, author

SERVING: Matthew 20:26-28   Romans 12:6-7   2 Corinthians 12:21
Galatians 5:13-14   Ephesians 6:7-8   1 Peter 4:10   1 Peter 5:2-4

November

19_____

SUN	MON	TUES	WED	THURS	FRI	SAT

*O, do not pray for easy lives. Pray to be stronger men.
Do not pray for tasks equal to your powers. Pray for powers
equal to your tasks.*
—*Phillip Brooks, 1835-1893, American religious leader*

Occasions for special prayer.

Ongoing prayer concerns.

BY ELISABETH *Thankfulness* ELLIOT

I was thankful...for the luxuries of modern American life—the speed of travel, the comfort of the seat (an economy-class airplane seat is infinitely more comfortable than the two boards at right angles which make up a "first class" seat on an Ecuadorian banana truck, and I've done my stint on those), the temperature of the cabin when outside it is perhaps seventy degrees below zero, the cleanliness, the quiet, the safety.

All these things, some cynic might point out, are relative. The Concorde travels much faster than a DC-10, a seat in first class is a lot roomier than one in economy class, it is sometimes frigid or stifling on planes, occasionally you find crumbs on your tray table and there is the chance of being seated next to some executive who has just had one of those three-martini lunches or some garrulous grandmother who wants to show you the latest Polaroids of the small person she has just visited. And planes crash, don't forget. So says the cynic.

But it is always possible to be thankful for what is given rather than to complain about what is not given. One or the other becomes a habit of life. There are, of course, complaints which are legitimate—as, for example, when services have been paid for which have not been rendered—but the gifts of God are in an altogether different category. Ingratitude to Him amounts (let us resort to no euphemisms) to rebellion.

Many women have told me that my husband's [martyred missionary, Jim Elliot] advice, which I once quoted in a book, has been an eye-opener to them. He said that a wife, if she is very generous, may allow that her husband lives up to perhaps eighty percent of her expectations. There is always the other twenty percent that she would like to change, and she may chip away at it for the whole of their married life without reducing it by very much. She may, on the other hand, simply decide to enjoy the eighty percent, and both of them will be happy. It's a down-to-earth illustration of a principle: Accept, positively and actively, what is given. Let thanksgiving be the habit of your life.

Such acceptance is not possible without a deep and abiding belief in the sovereign love of God. Either He is in charge, or He is not. Either He loves us, or He does not. If He is in charge and loves us, then whatever is given is subject to His control and is meant ultimately for our joy.

Elisabeth Elliot, *Love Has a Price Tag*, Christian Herald Books, 1979

❀

Personal response/goal:

_____

_____

_____

_____

_____

THANKFULNESS

November

*Bread of the world in
mercy broken,
Wine of the soul in
mercy shed,
By whom the words of
life were spoken,
And in whose death our
sins are dead!*

*Look on the heart by
sorrow broken,
Look on the tears by
sinners shed,
And be Thy feast to us
the token
That by Thy grace our
souls are fed.*

—Reginald Heber,
1783-1826, from the
hymn *Bread of the World
in Mercy Broken*

COMMUNION: Matthew 26:26-31   John 19–20   Luke 24:13-32   Acts 2:42-47
Acts 20:7-12   1 Corinthians 11:20-34

THANKFULNESS *November*

*If you can't be
thankful for what you
receive, be thankful
for what you escape.*

—Anonymous

_____

_____

_____

_____

_____

_____

_____

_____

_____

_____

_____

_____

_____

_____

_____

_____

_____

_____

_____

_____

_____

_____

_____

_____

_____

❋

ATTITUDE: Luke 17:7-19   Philippians 4:6-7   1 Thessalonians 5:18   Hebrews 2:1-4
Hebrews 12:28   2 Peter 1:4

November

We can choose to gather to our hearts the thorns of disappointment, failure, loneliness, and dismay due to our present situation, or we can gather the flowers of God's grace, unbounding love, abiding presence, and unmatched joy.

—Barbara Johnson,
   Stick a Geranium in Your Hat and Be Happy, Word Publishing, 1990

GRACE: John 1:1-17   Romans 3:22-24   Romans 5:15-20   Romans 6:14   Romans 11:6
1 Corinthians 15:10   2 Corinthians 9:8

T H A N K F U L N E S S
November

You want something but don't get it. You kill and covet, but you cannot have what you want. You quarrel and fight. You do not have, because you do not ask God.

James 4:2

❧

HINDRANCES: Psalm 22:1-2   Proverbs 1:24-31   Matthew 16:23   Luke 18:9-14
John 5:41-44   James 1:5-8   Jude 19

THANKFULNESS
November

"Lord, bless me,"
must always include the
prayerful willingness,
"Lord, use me."

—Janette Oke

SELFLESSNESS: Psalm 119:36   Ecclesiastes 2:4-11   John 8:5   2 Corinthians 9:12-15
Philippians 1:3-6   Philippians 2:3-4   James 3:13-18

THANKFULNESS *November*

For everything God created is good, and nothing is to be rejected if it is received with thanksgiving, because it is consecrated by the word of God and prayer.

1 Timothy 4:4-5

❧

POSSIBILITIES: Matthew 19:26   Mark 9:23   Romans 14:6-8   1 Corinthians 10:27-30
1 Corinthians 6:12   1 Corinthians 10:23-24   1 Timothy 4:1-5

[Brother Lawrence believed]

That the most excellent method
he had found of going to God
was that of doing our common
business without any view of
pleasing men, and (as far we are
capable) purely for the love of God.

That it was a great delusion to
think that the times of prayer ought
to differ from other times; that we
are as strictly obliged to adhere to
God by action in the time of action
as by prayer in the season of prayer.

That his prayer was nothing else
but a sense of the presence of God,
his soul being at that time insensible
to everything but divine love; and
that when the appointed times of
prayer were past, he found no difference, because he still continued
with God, praising and blessing
Him with all his might, so that he
passed his life in continual joy; yet
hoped that God would give him
somewhat to suffer when he should
grow stronger.

—Brother Lawrence, *The Practice of
the Presence of God*, Barbour and
Company, Inc., 1993

LIFESTYLE: Deuteronomy 5:28-29   Joshua 4:19-24   1 Chronicles 16:10-12   Psalm 34:1
Psalm 71:3, 14   Psalm 119:44, 132   Proverbs 28:14

THANKFULNESS

November

*Light is sweet, and it pleases
the eyes to see the sun.*

*However many years a man
may live, let him enjoy them all.*

Ecclesiastes 11:7-8a

_____

_____

_____

_____

_____

_____

_____

_____

_____

_____

_____

_____

_____

_____

_____

_____

_____

_____

_____

_____

_____

_____

_____

PLEASURE: Exodus 33:17   Psalm 16:6-11   Psalm 133:1   Psalm 135:3   Psalm 147:1
Romans 12:2   Romans 15:1-2

THANKFULNESS
November

I am oftimes driven to my knees by the overwhelming conviction that I have nowhere else to go.

—Abraham Lincoln, 1809-1865, 16th US President

NEEDS: Exodus 16:17-18   Deuteronomy 15:8   Isaiah 58:9-11   Matthew 25:36-40
2 Corinthians 9:12   Philippians 4:19   James 2:14-17

T H A *November* N E S S
THANKFULNESS

No ordinary meal—
a sacrament awaits us
   On our table spread.
   For men are risking lives
on sea and land
   That we may dwell in
safety and be fed.

—Grace from Scotland

❖

DAILY NEEDS: Job 23:12   Psalm 68:19   Matthew 6:11   Matthew 14:15-21
Colossians 3:17   Titus 3:14   Hebrews 3:13

THANKFULNESS

November

May the words of my mouth
and the meditation of my heart
be pleasing in your sight,
O Lord, my Rock and my Redeemer.

Psalm 19:14

    We all meditate throughout the
day on something. Whether it's
problems at work, or feelings about
a relationship gone sour, or trouble
with money, or good feelings of
thankfulness, love, and joy. What
is your heart meditating on,
and is it pleasing to God?

❁

MEDITATION: Joshua 1:8-9   Psalm 1:2   Psalm 48:9   Psalm 77:12   Psalm 104:34
Psalm 119:27, 48, 97   Psalm 143:5

*What is the word medita-
tion supposed to mean to us,
as those who have come into
communication with the Living
God through the One Way
He has opened up into His
presence?...Psalm 119:97:
"O how love I thy law! it is
my meditation all the day"
(KJV). Here is no special
position in which to put the
body, for this meditation is
taking place all the day, during
the time in which normal daily
life is being lived. Here is no
empty mind, no slowed-down
pulse—but a mind filled with
the content of God's law....
Never do I come to the end
of the possibility of meditating
upon that.*

—Edith Schaeffer, *A Way of
Seeing*, Fleming H. Revell
Publishing, 1977

FOCUS: Psalm 104:24-27 Psalm 145:14-17 Proverbs 19:23 Philippians 4:10-13
1 Timothy 6:6-10 Philemon 1:6 James 1:17

December

19_____

SUN	MON	TUES	WED	THURS	FRI	SAT

God has no problems—only plans. There is never panic in heaven.

—Corrie ten Boom

Occasions for special prayer.

_____

_____

_____

_____

_____

_____

_____

_____

Ongoing prayer concerns.

_____

_____

_____

_____

_____

_____

_____

_____

Detours

BY B.J. HOFF

Life's journey includes detours—
changed plans, failed dreams,
wrong-way turns, even dead ends.
Sometimes we feel abandoned,
left to wander in the wilderness
of defeat, discouragement, and despair.
But in His time, God steps in
to give Direction.

We often chafe when we're forced
to retreat or stand still and wait—
we want to advance.
But God knows we need training
and faith-building
and lessons in trust...
Discipline.

We strive to achieve, but God says, Learn.
We strain to run, but God says, Walk.
We struggle to do, but God says, Be...
And trust Me
with your Destination.

B.J. Hoff, *Faces in the Crowd*, Warner Press, Inc., 1993

Personal response/goal:

_____

_____

_____

_____

_____

_____

_____

_____

_____

_____

December

There are many things that appear trifles, which greatly tend to enervate the soul, and hinder its progress in the path to virtue and glory. The habit of indulging in things which our judgement cannot thoroughly approve, grows stronger and stronger by every act of self-gratification, and we are led on by degrees to an excess of luxury which must greatly weaken our hands in spiritual warfare.

—Margaret Woods, written 1771

BLESSING: Psalm 28:9   Psalm 29:11   Psalm 32:1-2   Psalm 118:26-29   Psalm 128
Matthew 5:3-12   Luke 24:50-53

December

D E T O U R S

God's promise were never meant to be thrown aside as waste paper. He intended that they should be used. God's gold is not miser's money, but is minted to be traded with. Nothing pleases our Lord better than to see His promises put into circulation; He loves to see His children bring them up to Him, and say, "Lord, do as You have said."

—Charles H. Spurgeon,
1834-1892, English preacher

DISCIPLINE: Proverbs 1:1-3   Proverbs 22:17-18   Proverbs 23:23   Acts 6:3-4
2 Timothy 1:7   Hebrews 2:1   2 Peter 1:19-21

December

We have grasped the mystery of the atom and rejected the Sermon on the Mount.

—Omar N. Bradley,
1893-1981, American
Army General

✺

WISDOM: 1 Kings 4:29-34   Matthew 12:42   Matthew 13:48-54   Luke 21:15
Acts 7:9-10   Romans 11:33-36   1 Corinthians 1:19-25

*The little babe may be
all that a babe could be,
or ought to be, and may
therefore perfectly please its
mother; and yet it is very far
from being what that mother
would wish it to be when the
years of maturity shall come.*

—Hannah Whitall Smith, *The
Christian's Secret of a Happy
Life*, Barbour and Company,
Inc., 1990

❀

MATURITY: Luke 8:14   1 Corinthians 2:6   Ephesians 4:11-15   Philippians 3:12-16
Colossians 4:12   Hebrews 5:11-14   James 1:4

December

In 1968, when our prayer experimentation started, several in our denomination were trained in Washington, D.C., for the Crusade of the Americas. We returned to our homes all excited over the prospects of prayer and evangelism. I said to my husband, "We're going to pray for a year and then we're going to evangelize for a year."

He grinned and announced, "It'll never work."

Jolted, I asked, "Why, not?"

He replied, "You show me somebody who's praying and I'll show you somebody who's evangelizing. A praying church is an evangelizing church."

He was right!

—Evelyn Christenson, *What Happens When Women Pray*, Victor Books, 1991

EVANGELISM: Matthew 9:31   Mark 1:43-45   Luke 2:16-20   John 8:25-26
John 12:1-18   Acts 5:17-20   Acts 6:7

Sacrifice and offering you did not desire, but my ears you have pierced;

burnt offerings and sin offerings you did not require.

Then I said, "Here I am, I have come—

It is written about me in the scroll.

I desire to do your will, O my God; your law is within my heart."

Psalm 40:6-8

OBEDIENCE: 1 Chronicles 21:19   2 Chronicles 31:21   Romans 5:19   Romans 6:16-19
2 Corinthians 9:13   Philemon 21   2 John 1:6

December

He, Who loved you unto
death, is speaking to you.
Listen, do not be deaf and
blind to Him. And as you
keep quiet and listen, you will
know, deep down in your
heart, that you are loved. As
the air is about you, so is His
love around about you now.

—Amy Carmichael,
    1867-1951, missionary to
    India and author

SOVEREIGN: 2 Samuel 7:18-22   Isaiah 40:10-11   Daniel 4:32   Amos 3:7-8
Zephaniah 1:7   Luke 2:25-35   Revelation 6:10

December

DETOURS

The shelter of Your love, Lord,
is my haven.
Freed from the struggle
of trying to fulfill my own dreams
and order my own life,
I can rest in Your arms
and be at peace.

—B.J. Hoff, *Faces in the Crowd*,
   Warner Press, 1993

_____

FULFILLMENT: Numbers 23:19   Joshua 21:45   1 Kings 8:24   Romans 13:8-10
Ephesians 1:9-10   2 Thessalonians 1:11   Revelation 17:17

Here I am, Lord;
Here is my body,
Here is my heart,
Here is my soul.
    Grant that I may be big enough to
reach the world,
    Strong enough to carry it,
    Pure enough to embrace it without
wanting to keep it.
    Grant that I may be a meeting-place,
but a temporary one,
    A road that does not end in itself,
    Because everything to be gathered there,
everything human,
    Leads toward You.

—Michel Quoist, *Prayers of Life,*
    Andrews and McMeel, Inc., 1985

OTHERS: Romans 2:17-24   Romans 11:17-21   Romans 12:3-8   1 Corinthians 9:24-27
1 Corinthians 10:24   Ephesians 4:29   Philippians 2:3-4

*May the favor of the Lord
our God rest upon us;
   establish the work of our
hands for us—
   yes, establish the work of
our hands.*

Psalm 90:17

❊

COMPLETE: John 3:29-30   John 15:11   John 16:24   John 17:23   Acts 20:24
Colossians 4:17   James 2:22-24

December

"His master replied, 'Well done, good and faithful servant'!"

Matthew 25:21

Lord, make me every moment aware of how much I want to hear You speak those words to me, when my time of serving You here is done.

ETERNITY: Psalm 93:2   Psalm 119:89, 160   Ecclesiastes 3:11   Isaiah 26:4
Daniel 4:3   Matthew 19:28-30   John 3:13-18

December

Lord, speak to me, that I may speak
In living echoes of Thy tone;
As Thou hast sought, so let me seek
The erring children lost and lone.

Oh! teach me, Lord, that I may teach
The precious things Thou dost impart;
And wing my words, that they may reach
The hidden depths of many a heart.

Oh! give Thine own sweet rest to me,
That I may speak with soothing pow'r
A word in season, as from Thee,
To weary ones in needful hour.

—Frances R. Havergal, 1836-1879, from the
   hymn *Lord, Speak to Me, That I May Speak*

WITNESS: Matthew 24:4-14   John 1:6-8   John 2:24-25   John 3:11   John 5:31-40
John 8:12-18   Acts 24:4-14

Personal Notes

Personal Notes

Personal Notes

PERSONAL NOTES

PERSONAL NOTES

Personal Notes

PERSONAL NOTES

PERSONAL NOTES

PERSONAL NOTES